X101

Restaurateur, writer an[...] [...]
was born in Liverpool [...]
Loughborough Univer[...]
where he gained a Ph.D[...]
co-proprietor of the Eve[...]
he spent the whole year in Japan, [...]
and Uechi-Ryu Karate. During his stay, he lived amongst
Japanese people and dined in many homes and restaurants
as well as doing a lot of cooking himself, using local methods
and ingredients. On his return in 1976, he opened a Karate
club in Liverpool.

David Scott

The
Japanese
Cookbook

line drawings by Steve Hardstaff

A MAYFLOWER BOOK

GRANADA

London Toronto Sydney New York

Abridged edition
Published by Granada Publishing Limited in 1981

ISBN 0 583 13218 9

First published in Great Britain in an unabridged form by
Barrie and Jenkins Ltd 1978
Copyright © David Scott 1978

Granada Publishing Limited
Frogmore, St Albans, Herts AL2 2NF
and
36 Golden Square, London W1R 4AH
866 United Nations Plaza, New York, NY 10017, USA
117 York Street, Sydney, NSW 2000, Australia
100 Skyway Avenue, Rexdale, Ontario, M9W 3A6, Canada
61 Beach Road, Auckland, New Zealand

Printed and bound in Great Britain
by Cox and Wyman Ltd, Reading
Set in Times

Granada ®
Granada Publishing ®

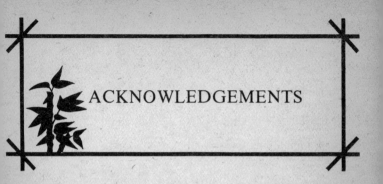

ACKNOWLEDGEMENTS

Many thanks to friends in Japan, particularly Yukinori, Akiko, Hirokazu and members of the Okinawan Uechi-Ryu Karate-Do Association. Special thanks to Jean for managing to decipher my handwriting, and for expertly typing the manuscript, and to Maire for her encouragement during the writing of the book. Finally, a special thanks to Nancy Duin, my editor, whose friendly and expert advice was invaluable throughout the preparation of *The Japanese Cookbook*.

CONTENTS

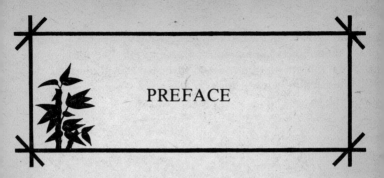

PREFACE

The prime aim of this book is to give a series of straightforward and, in the main, simple recipes for traditional Japanese meals. The book will be of value to anyone keen on cooking, and interested in preparing out-of-the-ordinary dishes. There are other Japanese cookery books, but I have generally found them not orientated to the Western cook. Too much emphasis has been placed on Classical Japanese cookery, and this often requires more time and special ingredients and skills than most people have. Thus there will be no recipes for elaborate festive meals, but there will be lots of authentic Japanese dishes of the sort prepared by the average Japanese housewife.

Grains, vegetables, seafood and fruit are the staple ingredients of the Japanese diet, and the emphasis in the recipes will be on these ingredients. However, meat and poultry are becoming more popular, especially in the cities, and recipes containing beef, pork and chicken are given.

The Japanese use very little oil in their cooking, and this, together with the low meat content of their diet, contributes to the very low incidence of heart disease in Japan. People on a low fat diet may find the book helpful in suggesting new ideas for their low fat meals.

Finally, a chapter in the book is devoted to Japanese-influenced macrobiotic cookery. The philosophy of Zen

Preface

Buddhism, and the traditional Japanese diet have contributed more than any other source to the food ideas of the macrobiotic movement, and this chapter will illustrate the connection between the two.

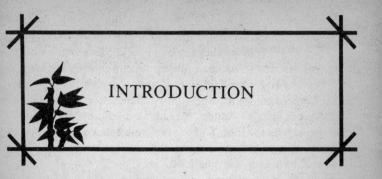

INTRODUCTION

About a thousand years ago, the Chinese gave the name Nippon to the group of islands we know as Japan. They believed this was the land that marked the end of the Eastern World. Here was where the sun rose out of the sea, and the name they gave to it means beginning of the sun.

In the Middle Ages the Fukien province of China, visited by Portuguese sailors on their way to Japan, was where the sailors picked up the local pronunciation of Nippon, and further corrupted it to Japao. Writing about this strange land, they described Japan as being so different from their homeland that it was the reverse of Europe.

The natives wore loose fitting smocks or kimonos. They ate lots of rice, vegetables, fish, fruit and sometimes the flesh of wild game. In contrast to the customs of the Western sailors, cleanliness was an important habit, especially at meal-times. Japanese society was complex, and many traditions were to be adhered to, much the same as it is today.

Tradition has been a major influence on Japanese cooking, and changes have been slow. In the fourteenth century under Zen Buddhist influence, aristocrats, monks and later ordinary folk stopped eating meat, and only in the last century has this started to change. The other influence on Japanese cooking has been Chinese cuisine, and many

Introduction

Japanese dishes have been inspired by the Chinese.

Like the Chinese, the Japanese serve dishes in much smaller amounts than their Western counterparts, but they do serve a larger variety. In the preparation of the dishes, each ingredient is valued for its taste, appearance and freshness. Bowls, dishes, utensils are chosen for their harmony with the food, and this is always eaten with hashi or wooden chopsticks, since wood is thought to be the material most in harmony with the food.

You do not require special equipment or skills to serve authentic Japanese meals; all you need to do is take care over the preparation of all the various dishes, e.g. clean the vegetables extra thoroughly, cut them especially neatly, etc. Choose your favourite room, and around a low table in the middle, lay a cushion for each guest.

With good company, your favourite crockery, chopsticks and a respect for the food to be eaten, you have all you need to create the harmony and pleasure of a true Japanese dinner.

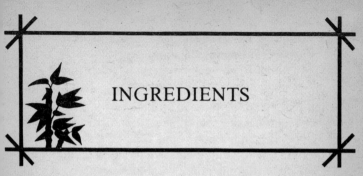

INGREDIENTS

Sea Vegetables

Sea vegetables or seaweeds are the Japanese food West-
erners are most likely to be prejudiced against, yet in Britain
laver bread and other seaweed dishes have been made for
centuries. In Japan seaweeds as foodstuffs are common-
place, and their use is taken for granted. In fact kombu
seaweed is packaged in fancy boxes which are given as
presents by appreciative guests when they go to dinner.

As with land vegetables, the environment of the area in
which the seaweed grows affects its quality and taste, but
seaweeds are usually rich in vitamins and minerals, they are
easily digestible, and provide a good protein source. Perhaps
as we exhaust our other food sources they will become more
popular. Apart from their nutritive value, they are very
useful for seasoning, and this is the way seaweeds are most
often used in Japan.

Nori, hijiki and kombu are the types of seaweed usually
available in shops in the West. Nori seaweed is dried, pressed
into sheets, and wrapped around rolls of rice to make a sort
of Japanese sandwich called norimaki. Crumbled over rice
or soups nori adds a distinctive flavour. Hijiki is cooked with
soya sauce, and eaten as a side dish, and it's also good in
salads or fried rice. Perhaps kombu is best known as a
basic constituent of dashi or Japanese soup stock, but it can

also be used to garnish rice dishes, to season vegetables, and
in a variety of other ways.

Fish

Japan, surrounded on all sides by the sea, is a great fish-
eating nation. In the interior of the country, fish is more
scarce, but even here most people eat some fish every day. To
satisfy this demand, the Japanese fishing fleets visit waters
all over the world. Sadly, their catch still includes the whale,
but hopefully with increased world pressure this will stop.
The trawlers travel far from home, but the waters around
Japan are blessed with fish of all kinds, and the Japanese
seem to have mastered the art of cooking each type in the
most suitable way. In fact it's possible to have a fine and
interesting Japanese meal that contains fish in every course
including the dessert!

Fish stories are part of the folklore of Japan, and sashimi
or raw fish is part of the folklore of Western attitudes to the
Japanese diet. However, contrary to popular imagination,
sashimi neither tastes nor smells fishy; it has its own subtle
flavour which people usually appreciate once they have
tasted it. I wasn't sure whether to include recipes for sashimi
in this book, because I do agree that outside the environment
of Japan, eating raw fish seems an unlikely thing to do, but
trusting to the experimental nature of the reader, I have
included information on the preparation of sashimi. These
dishes, along with other fish recipes in the book, can be
prepared with the sorts of fish available at the local
fishmonger.

Vegetables and Vegetable Cutting Techniques

The Japanese are very appreciative of vegetables, and great
care is taken to ensure they are cooked in a manner which
retains the different textures and flavours of the various
types. They eat more vegetables and less meat than we do in
the West, and grow a greater variety. Whether through good

luck or good management, their vegetables are of the best quality, and the average Japanese greengrocery shop, with its display of crispy, clean, shiny and delicious-looking vegetables, looks more like a stand at a horticulture show.

Vegetables are not seen as an accompaniment to a main dish, but as an independent part of the meal. They are not generally served plain, but seasoned with soya sauce, miso, sesame seeds, or other ingredients such as tofu. The vegetables are only lightly cooked, and the Japanese make little distinction between salads and vegetables, which are anyway sometimes served cold. Pickled vegetables may be substituted where we may use salads. The vegetables are either cooked quickly in a little oil, or sautéed first and then simmered in a drop of water. Leafy green vegetables and others that contain a lot of water are cooked in their own liquid in a pan with a heavy lid.

Below is a list of vegetables commonly used in Japan. The list is divided into three sections. The first section will be familiar, and contains those vegetables easily available in our own shops. The second includes vegetables not as easy to obtain fresh, but usually on sale at specialist shops, or Indian, West Indian or Chinese grocery stores. The third list is made up of distinctively Japanese vegetables with their English names. Some of the vegetables are available canned, and the others where they appear in recipes will be included as optional ingredients. A brief description of these unusual vegetables is given beneath the lists.

I
Aubergines (egg plants)
Bell peppers
Broccoli
Cucumber
Carrots
Cabbage

Celery
French beans
Lettuce
Leeks
Mushrooms
Onions
Peas
Potatoes
Spring onions
Sprouts
Tomatoes
Turnips

II

Asparagus
Bean sprouts
Chinese cabbage
Corn on the cob
Okra
Pumpkin
Sweet potatoes

III

Daikon – Japanese radish
Gobo – Burdock root
Renkon – Lotus root
Shiitake – Dried mushroom
Shungiku – Chrysanthemum leaves
Takenoko – Bamboo shoots

Daikon – Japanese white radish, it grows to a foot (30 cm) or more in length, and can be used fresh or pickled. Small sweet turnips make a fair substitute.

Gobo – This is the long, slender root vegetable, burdock. Peeled and chopped into matchstick shapes, it is used extensively in Japanese cookery.

Renkon – Lotus root is a white sausage-shaped vegetable. Sliced thinly cross-wise, it gives beautiful white slices patterned symmetrically with small holes. The taste is somewhat bland.

Shiitake – Japanese tree mushrooms are cultivated by injecting fungus into the soft barks of water-soaked tree trunks. The mushrooms are dried before being sold. They are quite expensive and the very best varieties are a delicacy only the rich can afford. Large fresh mushrooms or French champignons can sometimes be substituted.

Shungiku – The edible leaves of the chrysanthemum plant impart a subtle fragrance to soups and casseroles. Spinach has the same colour and texture, but it has a stonger flavour, and, if used as a replacement, it should be added carefully in small amounts.

Takenoko – Bamboo shoots are normally only available canned; however, the crisp texture even of the canned variety makes a contrast to soft cooked vegetables.

Vegetable Cutting
In a Japanese kitchen the cutting board is as important as the stove. Vegetables are cut to suit the manner in which they are to be cooked, and each type of vegetable is cut in a uniform fashion to ensure uniform cooking of each piece. An additional factor to be borne in mind is that the meal is to be eaten with chopsticks, and each piece should be small enough to pick up and put into the mouth whole. Further, it is important that the appearance of the cooked or uncooked vegetables should be pleasing to the eye. Following are sketches of various methods of cutting up vegetables: some are obvious, others may be new to you. There are of course many other techniques, and you may wish to use your own cutting methods to produce other interesting shapes.

Circle Cutting (Wa-Giri)

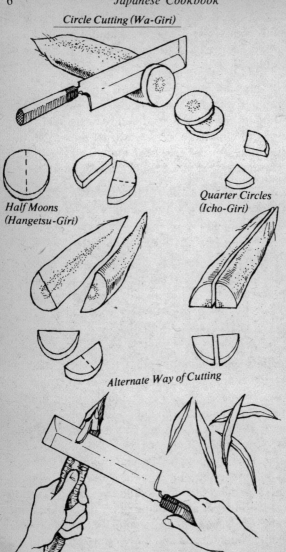

Half Moons
(Hangetsu-Giri)

Quarter Circles
(Icho-Giri)

Alternate Way of Cutting

Pencil Cutting (Sasagaki)

Cutting into Rectangles (Tanzaku-Giri)

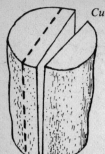
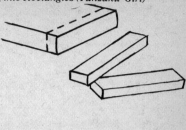

Cutting Rectangles into Thick Strips and Chopping Coarsely (Sainome-Giri)

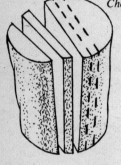
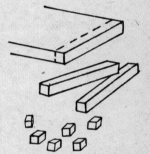
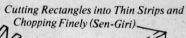

Cutting Rectangles into Thin Strips and Chopping Finely (Sen-Giri)

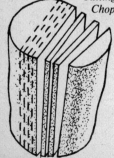
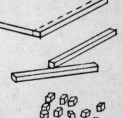

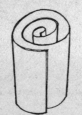

Cutting on the Bias

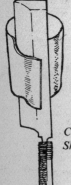

Cutting into Thin Sheets or Bark Shapes (Katsura-Muki)

Chrysanthemum Cutting (Kikka-Kabu)

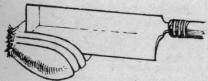

Onion Dicing (Mijin-Giri)

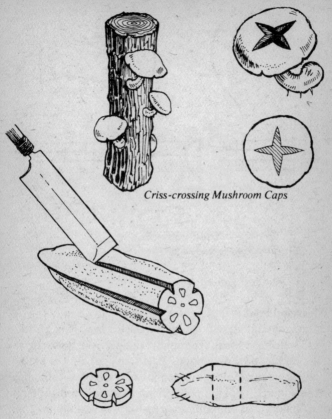

Criss-crossing Mushroom Caps

Cutting into Flower Shapes (Hanagata)

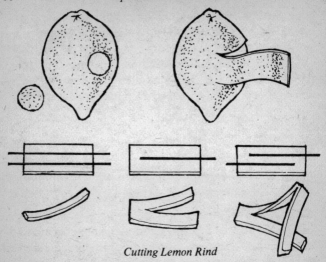

Cutting Lemon Rind

Meat and Poultry

Meat, especially beef, is very expensive in Japan, and it is
used sparingly. Steak is popular, but only in restaurants, and
it is rarely cooked at home. Beef steak, when it is used, is
cooked in very thin slices as part of a sukiyaki-type meal.
Where quick cooking is required, pre-cooked meat is cut
into small cubes and combined with rice or vegetables. There
is nothing in the Japanese diet analogous to the Sunday
roast. The meat is, however, of good quality, and beef from
the Kobe area of Japan, where they include beer in the cattle
diet, is justly famous. Kobe steakhouses are popular all over
Japan, even though they sell in total much more steak than
the area around Kobe could possibly supply.

Keeping pigs needs much less space than keeping the same
number of cows and this has meant with Japan's land
shortage that pork is more often a part of the Japanese diet

than beef. Again, it is eaten sparingly, although bacon is becoming popular, and a bacon and egg breakfast is quite common amongst young people.

Chicken, next to fish, is the animal food most important in Japanese cookery. Other types of fowl are not well-known, although wild game occasionally appears on the menu.

Seasonings

We have already mentioned shoyu, miso and seaweeds are used as seasonings in Japanese cookery, and the ingredients below complete the list of condiments commonly used by the Japanese cook.

Sesame Seeds (Goma) – Sesame seeds are toasted and then crushed to be used as a seasoning on their own or mixed with salt. This salt mixture is called gomashiso. Sesame seed oil is sometimes added to soya or corn cooking oil, to give a nutty flavour to the cooked food.

Vinegar – Vinegar is called for in a number of recipes. The Japanese use a distilled rice wine that gives a slightly sweet vinegar. Cider vinegar is a suitable substitute.

Mirin – Mirin is a sweet fortified wine, used to sweeten and glaze. Sherry or a sweetened white wine are alternatives.

Aji-No-Moto – This is a seasoning based on monosodium glutamate. It is tasteless, but brings out the flavour of foods. Excessive use can cause stomach trouble, and I have not specified its use in any of the recipes.

Ginger Root (Shoga) – Sliced or grated ginger root is eaten on its own, raw, or pickled as a side dish. It is also used as a spice in cooking, and it has the property of absorbing fishy smells if added to the fish before cooking.

Wasabi – Japanese horse-radish mustard is used in dipping sauces, and in the preparation of sushi rice balls. It is sold in powder form in the same way as English mustard, a fair replacement.

Togarashi – A blend of several spices, which when combined taste like a mixture of black pepper and hot pepper sauce. Either or both the latter can be substituted, but use sparingly.

Dried Bonito (Katsuobushi) – The soup stock dashi, used as the base for various Japanese dishes, is prepared by boiling together flakes of the dried bonito fish called katsuobushi and kombu seaweed. It is possible to buy packets of bonito flakes, but in Japan they sell the dried bonito fish whole. The dried fish looks like a combination between a truncheon and a boomerang, and it's as hard as both. On one occasion, scraping flakes off these hard sticks I almost lost a finger, and I wouldn't recommend trying it, not, that is, if you can find a packet of the pre-flaked fish.

There are other soup stocks just as suitable as dashi, and easier to prepare, and since the ingredients for dashi are not readily available in the West recipes for both dashi and substitutes are given.

A complete glossary of Japanese cookery terms is given at the end of the book.

Tea and Sake

Green tea or o-cha is drunk on every conceivable occasion. Wherever you go in Japan you will see work people drinking tea from large metal teapots filled with warm o-cha. It's served free in restaurants and snack bars. Tea is drunk without milk or sugar. Powdered green tea is also used to flavour foods such as noodles and ice-cream.

Sake, the light rice wine, is also served on any occasion. It is poured from a sake jug into tiny cups and sipped. Warm sake is served in the winter. It is also used extensively in cooking – white wine or dry sherry may be used as a substitute.

Tea and sake are discussed in greater detail in the chapter on beverages.

KITCHEN
EQUIPMENT

You will need very little special equipment for Japanese cookery, and most of the recipes given could be followed adequately in an ordinarily equipped Western kitchen, but to increase your joy in Japanese cooking, and to make the job easier, the following items will be helpful:

Hocha – A Japanese all-purpose cutting knife, with a squared-off end. They are excellent for cutting vegetables.

Cutting Board – A thick, unvarnished, heavy chopping board makes all types of cutting jobs easier, and reduces the risk of cut fingers.

Saibashi – Long cooking chopsticks used for handling hot foods, and mixing ingredients at the stove. They are wooden, taper to a point at the end, and are usually joined at the other end by a piece of string.

Saucepans – Heavy duty pans with good fitting lids are the most useful for boiling rice, making soups, sautéing, vegetables, etc. At home I have a series of heavy wooden lids that are just laid on top of the saucepan. They are interchangeable between pans, and reversed on a work top they make extra chopping boards.

Sudare – A flexible rolling mat constructed of fine bamboo slats, it is used for preparing sushi rice rolls. It's possible to find bamboo squares designed for use as table mats that make a good substitute.

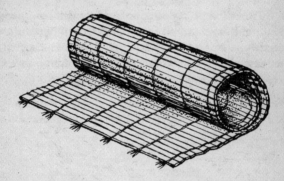

Surikogi and Suribachi – A mortar and pestle. The bowl is earthenware and serrated inside. With the wooden pestle it is effective for grinding sesame seeds, pulses, making purées, etc.

Zaru – A bamboo strainer which doubles as a colander for draining foods, and as a container for serving food at the table. An ordinary colander and a wicker bread basket will do the jobs separately.

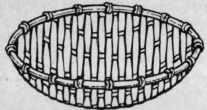

Wok – This Chinese cooking pot is excellent for quick or deep frying. It is fitted with a wooden lid for simmering food, and with one or more bamboo steaming baskets that sit inside the wok one on top of the other, different dishes may be steamed. The wok has a rounded base, and to give it stability on an ordinary gas stove, it is worthwhile using a wok support.

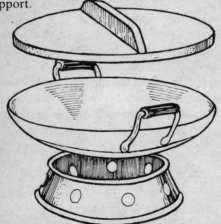

Finally, for cooking meals at the table, an electric frying pan is very useful. Alternatively, use a table-top gas burner of the type used by camping enthusiasts.

RECIPE NOTES

The recipes were prepared with authenticity as a prime consideration, but where a preferred ingredient is specialist, a viable alternative has been suggested. Recipes that include ingredients very difficult to obtain outside Japan have not been included.

The following points are applicable to the recipe section in general, and I have listed them here to save repeating them in each individual recipe.

Before starting a recipe, read the notes at the beginning of the chapter in which it appears. There may be useful information applicable to the recipe.

Where the recipe stipulates the use of a pan, you may also use a wok. If the ingredients list mushrooms, this means ordinary fresh mushrooms. Where shiitake are stipulated, Japanese dried tree mushrooms are required (see glossary for alternatives).

Fresh ginger root is called for in a number of recipes. This is now quite generally available, but when you cannot obtain any, ground ginger used sparingly may be used as a replacement. 2 parts ginger powder equals 1 part root ginger.

The best method to steam food is with a wok and Chinese bamboo steamer, but if you do not have this equipment, use the following method. Put 2.5 cm (1 in) water in a large pot, bring to the boil, and carefully place in the pot an inverted bowl. On top of the bowl lay a plate containing the food to be steamed. Cover the mouth of the pot with a clean tea towel, place on the lid and steam at medium heat. The cloth prevents moisture dripping on to the food. A small colander that will fit inside the pot can be used in place of the bowl and plate.

Seaweeds and shiitake are usually only available, in the West, dried. In some recipes they are used in the dried form, and in others pre-soaked. Where the reconstituted variety are required this will be stipulated, otherwise use dried. To reconstitute dried vegetables, soak in warm water approximately 30 minutes. Reserve the soaking liquid for use in stocks, etc.

Sesame seeds appear quite often in Japanese recipes. They are used either whole or partially ground and roasted. To roast the seeds, heat a heavy frying pan on a medium flame. When the pan is hot enough to evaporate a drop of water instantly, add the seeds and reduce the heat. Shake the pan about, and keep the seeds moving around. They are ready after about three minutes, and should be light brown in colour. Store in a glass jar, and grind as required. A pepper mill will grind small amounts, but for larger quantities use a suribachi and surikogi or pestle and mortar. Where it is more convenient, tahini may be substituted for ground sesame seeds. ½ tablespoon tahini equals 1 tablespoon ground sesame seeds.

Bamboo shoots and lotus roots are required in some of the recipes. They are not generally available fresh, and the recipes always refer to the tinned variety.

French beans are frequently used as a garnishing. They should always be topped, tailed and stringed before use, unless young and fresh. Dwarf French beans, green beans and runner beans may also be used.

Nori seaweed is another popular garnishing. It is sold in paper-thin sheets and for garnishing purposes is usually lightly toasted before use. To toast, wave a sheet of nori over a medium flame or hot electric ring for 30–40 seconds or until crisp and crumbly.

To ease the shelling of prawns and shrimps, drop them into boiling water for one or two minutes before shelling.

The ingredients listed below are basic to the recipes described in this book, and a stock of these ingredients or their alternatives available in the kitchen will be very useful when using the book.

Sesame seeds
Ginger root
Soy sauce (Tamari variety)
Sake or medium dry white wine
Mirin or medium sweet sherry
Cider or mild white vinegar
Young leeks or spring onions or chives or scallions or shallots, all to be used as garnishings
Soup stock, fish or vegetable, or bouillon cubes

Weights and Measures

Quantities in recipes have been given in both metric and imperial measures.

The following table was used for the conversion of imperial to metric:

Ounces/Fluid Ounces	Grammes or Millilitres to the nearest unit of 25
1	25
2	50
3	75
4	100
5	150
6	175
7	200
8	225
9	250
10	275
11	300
12	350
13	375
14	400
15	425
16	450
17	475
18	500
19	550
20	575

5 fl oz	=	¼ pt	=	150 ml
10 fl oz	=	½ pt	=	275 ml
20 fl oz	=	1 pt	=	575 ml
35 fl oz	=	1¾ pt	=	1 l
16 oz	=	1 lb	=	450 g
2 lb 3 oz	=	1 kg		

For American readers the following conversions for liquid measurements may be useful.

Imperial	American
8 pt	10 pt
2 pt	5 cups
16 fl oz	1 pt
1 pt	2½ cups
8 fl oz	1 cup
2 fl oz = 4 tablespoons	¼ cup
½ fl oz = 1 tablespoon	approx 1½ tablespoons
1 teaspoon = ¼ tablespoon	1 teaspoon = ⅓ tablespoon

For small amounts of ingredients tablespoon measurements have been used in the recipes. If you prefer to weigh things out, the following table lists commonly used ingredients with their tablespoon measurements and equivalent weight or volume amounts.

Salt, sake, vinegar, soy sauce, miso, mirin	1 teaspoon	⅕ oz	5 g
Salt, sake, vinegar oil	1 tablespoon	¾ oz	20 g
Sugar, cornflour, flour	1 tablespoon	½ oz	15 g
Soy sauce, miso, mirin	1 tablespoon	1 oz	28 g

Bear in mind that there are so many variables in cooking that it is not possible to be exactly precise about every weight and volume. Much depends on personal taste and judgement, and you are your own best judge of when a particular seasoning is just right or when a particular dish is cooked to your liking.

Serving and Planning a Japanese Meal

If you are planning a Japanese dinner, and not experimenting with a single dish, the following advice will help you do it in genuine style.

First of all, don't buy too much of any one ingredient, but

buy the best quality and freshest specimens you can find or afford. Persuade your grocer or fishmonger to select for you the choicest of his stock of vegetables or fish. Plan a menu that is nutritively well balanced. Meat and/or fish, but not too much, cooked vegetables, fresh or pickled vegetables, rice and fresh fruit. Concentrate on eye appeal, and go to some trouble arranging the food before serving. There is no rigid serving order, but generally all the dishes are laid on the table at the same time, and the hot dishes eaten first. A sensible system for the host who wishes to join the guests during the meal.

How you serve the meal will depend to some extent on the type and quantity of crockery you have, but ideally you need for each person: bowls for soup and rice, small plates for pickles and other titbits, a bowl each for the main courses, wooden chopsticks and small Japanese or Chinese teacups.

Except for whole fish, the food is cut into mouth-sized pieces, either before or after cooking, whichever is the most suitable. The dishes that compose the meal are served for each guest in the various bowls, and then taken to the table. Before starting the meal remind your guests to say to you '*Itadakimasu*' to which you reply '*Dozo*', or roughly translated, 'I would like to begin this fine meal'; reply 'Oh please do'.

Allow older people to start first, and if a bowl is passed to you take it in both hands as a mark of respect for the food it contains. If you take food from a communal bowl, reverse your chopsticks, and use the blunt end for removing the chosen morsel. If you are going to want more rice, leave a few grains in the bottom of your bowl. This is the signal, and if your guests do the same, pass them the rice. However, when you have had enough rice, clean the bowl free of all rice grains, otherwise legend has it that you will develop a rash of warts! One thing to remember, if you have a large appetite: it is considered impolite to start first and finish last. At the end of the meal, place your chopsticks neatly on the table (or chopstick rests) not in the bowl. If you have primed your guests sufficiently well, they may say to you '*Arigato Gozaimashito*' or 'Thank you for an excellent dinner'. Finally, do remember to keep the teapot topped up with hot water, and the sake cups well filled.

I haven't tried to explain how to use chopsticks. It seems to me more difficult to follow complicated instructions than to pick up a pair and experiment. Just remember one stick stays stationary, and the other moves. Chopsticks do add an extra quality to eating a Japanese meal so, if you cannot yet use them, I hope you will persevere in your efforts.

SOUPS
AND STOCKS

One of the things that most surprised me when I arrived in Japan was the custom of having miso soup for breakfast, but I discovered that it was quick to prepare, nutritious and warming on a cold morning. By the time I had established myself in my own apartment, I had begun to start the day with my bowl of miso soup.

Miso soup, along with many other Japanese soups is based on an all-purpose soup stock called dashi. This is made from dried bonito fish flakes and kombu seaweed. In Japan dashi is a quick and economical stock to make. The ingredients are easily available and cheap. This is not usually the case in the West, and while giving a recipe for dashi, I have also given recipes for chicken, fish and vegetable stocks, which may be substituted for it. Your own ideas and variations on the preparation of soup stock will add a different flavour and greater usefulness to those soup recipes that require a stock base.

The Japanese, as we do, divide their soups into roughly two types. One category is clear soups or suimono, which are appreciated for the distinctiveness, colour and quality of their garnishings, while the second category, the thick soups or sumashi-shiru, is more akin to the Western stew. Most of the sumashi-shiru contain miso as an ingredient. Just as we tend to be casual about the ingredients of a stew, so do the

Japanese, and once you have established the taste and style of the thicker soups, you do not need to adhere strictly to the ingredients listed in recipes.

The two categories of soups of course overlap, and I have found it more convenient and practical to divide the soup recipes into clear soups, soups that do not contain miso, and miso soups. The former recipes are given first.

Soups that contain noodles as a major ingredient will be found in the chapter on noodles.

The quantities given in the soup recipes are for four servings. If, however, the soup dish is only part of a large meal, the amount prepared will stretch to six servings. It is convenient to make large amounts of soup stock and the quantities given for stocks are sufficient to prepare enough for two soup recipes.

Soup Stocks

Dashi

20 g (¾ oz) kombu seaweed
2 l (4 pt) water
20 g (¾ oz) bonito flakes (katsuobushi)
Soy sauce to taste (optional)

Clean the seaweed with a damp cloth, then add it to the water and bring to the boil. Boil for three to four minutes, turn down heat and remove, but reserve seaweed. Add the bonito flakes. Re-heat, and as the water just returns to the boil turn off the heat. Leave to stand for five minutes or until the bonito sinks. Strain, reserving the bonito for further use. Season with soy sauce and the dashi is ready for use.

To prepare a weaker stock for cooking vegetables, the reserved seaweed and bonito fish flakes may be boiled for ten minutes in 850 ml (1½ pt) water. The secondary dashi is strained off and the bonito and kombu are discarded.

Chicken Stock

This is not a fixed recipe and you may use other vegetables apart from those listed.

900 g (2 lb) chicken bones or leftover chicken pieces
100 g (4 oz) cabbage, shredded
100 g (4 oz) carrots, grated
100 g (4 oz) leeks, sliced
100 g (4 oz) celery, chopped
2 l (4 pt) water
Salt and/or soy sauce to taste

Chop the chicken bones into convenient-size pieces and put all the ingredients, except the seasoning, into a pan. Bring to the boil, and then simmer for an hour or more. Occasionally, skim off the fat and other residues that float to the surface. Strain and season the reserved stock to taste.

Fish Stock

450 g (1 lb) head, tail and other trimmings of any white fish
1 medium onion, diced
50 g (2 oz) finely chopped, fresh ginger root
2 l (4 pt) water
Salt and/or soy sauce to taste

Put all the ingredients, except the seasoning, in a pan. Bring to the boil and cook for 20–30 minutes. Remove any scum that floats to the surface. Strain and season the reserved stock to taste.

Vegetable Stock

This recipe is not fixed and you may use any combination of the suggested vegetables or any others you think suitable.

With stocks nothing need be wasted, and you can use vegetable trimmings, the good parts of partly bad vegetables, etc.

175 g (6 oz) soya beans, soaked overnight and drained
2 l (4 pt) water
Soy sauce, salt and black pepper or togarashi to taste
½ teaspoon yeast extract (optional)
Any three or four of the following chopped vegetables, total weight 450 g (1 lb): carrots, turnips, parsnips, celery, potatoes, onions, cabbage, cauliflower.

Place all the vegetables in one pan, add the water and drained beans. Bring to the boil, simmer for two to three hours. Strain off the stock and season.

Clear Soups (and Soups without Miso)
Most of the soups call for soup stock. If you do not have any available, or the time to prepare any, chicken or vegetable bouillon cubes can be used.

Clear Soup With Garnishings

This soup is served in individual bowls, each containing a few tiny pieces of colourful garnishings. It is served with the meal. Chopsticks are used to pick out the garnishings, and the soup is then sipped directly from the bowl.

1 l (2 pt) clear vegetable soup stock
2 tablespoons soy sauce
Garnishings (see recipe and table below)
Salt to taste

The stock and soy sauce are heated together and seasoned to taste with salt. The soup is poured into the bowls, and the garnishings added. Three items different in texture and shape should be used. For something solid use a piece of

cooked noodle, diced omelette or tofu; add something
delicate and leafy, say a celery leaf or parsley sprig; and
finally a carefully cut piece of vegetable, such as a thin slice
of carrot or mushroom, chopped spring onion or sliced
French bean.

There are many other suitable garnishings and I have
suggested some below:

SOLID
Boiled egg
Cooked meat
Cooked fish
Peanuts
Small dumplings
Shellfish

LEAFY
Watercress
Cucumber
Leek
Spinach
Chinese cabbage
Chrysanthemum leaves

VEGETABLE
Potato (cooked)
Daikon or turnip
Onion
Bean sprouts
Green pepper
Aubergine

Select one ingredient from each column and cut into delicate
shape and size. Add to the clear soup stock as directed
above.

Clear Soup With Rice Dumplings

2 tablespoons vegetable oil
1 medium turnip, diced
2 leaves Chinese cabbage, 2.5 cm (1 in) wide strips
1 l (2 pt) clear soup stock or dashi
Salt to taste
25 g (1 oz) parsley, chopped
225 g (8 oz) rice flour
150 ml (5 fl oz) water, boiling

Sauté the diced turnips in the oil in a heavy saucepan until just soft. Stir in the Chinese cabbage and pour in the stock. Bring to the boil, and then simmer for twenty minutes. While the soup is cooking, prepare the rice dumplings. Carefully add boiling water to the rice flour whilst stirring vigorously with a wooden spoon. Add as much water as necessary to produce quite a stiff dough. Knead the dough for three or four minutes, and then remove small portions and roll into dumplings. Season the cooked soup with salt and drop in the dumplings. Initially they will drop to the bottom of the pan, but as they cook through (two to three minutes) they will rise to the surface. Serve and garnish each bowl with a little parsley.

Clear Soup With Fish Dumplings

2 tablespoons vegetable oil
1 medium parsnip, cut in matchsticks
1 medium carrot, sliced thinly
1 l (2 pt) clear soup stock or dashi
100 g (4 oz) fillet white fish (or tinned sardine, salmon)
25 g (1 oz) ginger root, finely grated (optional)
2 small spring onions, finely chopped
1 egg white
3 tablespoons flour

1 small bunch watercress, chopped
Salt to taste

Sauté the parsnips and carrot in the oil in a heavy pan until just soft. Cover with stock, bring to the boil, then simmer for twenty minutes. While the soup is cooking prepare the fish dumplings. Grind the fish to a smooth paste in a suribachi or mortar, mix in the ginger root, spring onion and egg white. Carefully blend in the flour until the mixture is stiff enough to form into small dumplings. Season the cooked stock with salt, drop in the dumplings and simmer until cooked through (three to four minutes). Add the watercress and serve immediately.

Clear Soup With Flower-Shaped Prawns

This is a very Japanese-looking soup. It is a little exotic, but worth the trouble for special occasions.

8 prawns
2 tablespoons cornflour
4 shiitake, pre-soaked in cold water
  (or 4 fresh mushrooms)
8 stalks asparagus, cut into 5 cm (2 in) pieces
1 l (2 pt) clear soup stock or dashi
1 tablespoon mirin or sweet sherry (optional)
Rind of 1 medium lemon

Shell prawns, leaving the tails intact. Make a shallow cut along the outside curve of each prawn and carefully remove the black vein. Now make a small slit in the middle of the body and squeeze the tail through. Pull it out the other side to give the flower shape. Lightly sprinkle the prawns with cornflower. Bring the stock to the boil, add the prawns and shiitake or mushrooms. Reduce heat and simmer until prawns are cooked. Cook the asparagus lengths in lightly salted water. Drain. Add the mirin or sweet sherry to the soup. Divide the asparagus and soup into four bowls and garnish with lemon rind.

Chicken and Leek Soup

450 g (1 lb) boiling chicken
1 l (2 pt) water
3 peppercorns
1 tablespoon soy sauce
Salt to taste
Juice of 1 lemon
1–2 leeks, sliced
50 g (2 oz) somen or vermicelli noodles

Chop the chicken into four pieces and bring to boil in water with peppercorns, soy sauce and salt to taste. Simmer until chicken meat is tender. Skim off rising scum and strain. Reserve both liquid and chicken. Remove meat from the bones and cut into small pieces. Return liquid to pan and skim off fat from the surface. Add lemon juice, leeks and return to the boil. Add the chicken and simmer until leeks are just cooked. Meanwhile, cook somen noodles in boiling salted water until soft (approximately five minutes). Put a portion of somen in each bowl and pour over the chicken and leek soup.

Egg Drop Soup

By swirling the soup around as you pour in the beaten egg, you can form beautiful patterns with the strands of cooked egg. The Japanese call these shapes egg-flowers.

2 eggs, beaten
1 tablespoon sake or sweet white wine (optional)
1 pinch of salt
1 l (2 pt) clear soup stock or dashi
2 teaspoons cornflour
1 teaspoon soy sauce
4 small leaves spinach, chopped
4 sprigs parsley

Whisk the eggs, add the sake and pinch of salt. Mix the cornflour to a smooth paste with a little of the cold stock. Bring stock to the boil, pour in the paste and stir in. Add soy sauce and season with salt to taste. Now gradually add beaten egg stirring constantly. Bring to the boil, add spinach and turn off heat. Pour into soup bowls and garnish with parsley.

Summertime Egg Soup

4 eggs
1 l (2 pt) water
1 pinch salt
3 tablespoons vinegar
1 medium cucumber, peeled and diced
100 g (4 oz) peas, fresh or tinned
1 l (2 pt) vegetable soup stock
Rind 1 lemon

Place the water, vinegar and pinch of salt in a pan and bring to the boil. Lower the heat and poach the eggs one by one. Reserve the cooked eggs in warm water. While the eggs are cooking bring the stock to the boil, add the vegetables and simmer until cooked. Place one egg in each bowl, pour over the hot soup and garnish with lemon peel.

Shrimp Soup

> 175 g (6 oz) fresh shrimps, peeled, finely chopped
> 1 egg, beaten
> 175 g (6 oz) daikon, finely diced (small sweet turnip may
>   be substituted)
> 1 pinch salt
> 1 l (2 pt) clear soup stock or dashi
> 4 shiitake, soaked and softened, or 100 g (4 oz)
>   mushrooms
> 4 spinach leaves

Combine the shrimps, egg, radish and pinch of salt. Boil
stock, add mushrooms and simmer for five minutes. Add
spinach, cook for further two minutes. Divide shrimp
mixture between four bowls. Ladle two mushrooms and a
spinach leaf into each bowl and pour over hot stock.

Pork and Vegetable Soup

> 225 g (8 oz) lean pork, thin slices
> 1 l (2 pt) clear soup stock or dashi
> 2 small carrots, sliced thinly
> 150 g (5 oz) tinned bamboo shoots, sliced thinly into half-
>   moon shapes
> 8 shiitake, soaked and drained (optional)
> 2 leaves Chinese or white cabbage
> 25 g (1 oz) ginger root, grated
> Salt, soy sauce to taste
> 2 spring onions, finely chopped

Cut pork into 2.5 cm (1 in) squares. Boil stock, add pork and
cook for five minutes. Add all the other ingredients except
seasoning and spring onions. Return to the boil, reduce heat
and simmer for five minutes. Season and serve, garnished
with spring onions.

Thick Rice Soup

Once sitting in a café in Okinawa, I was intrigued by the cast-iron soup bowl, with a wooden lid, laid on the table in front of the man next to me. When he took the lid off I was more interested in the contents, a steaming bowl of rice soup.

    1 l (2 pt) clear soup stock or dashi
    75 g (3 oz) rice
    25 g (1 oz) ginger root, grated
    Salt and black pepper or togarashi to taste
    100 g (4 oz) peas (fresh or tinned)
    1 sheet nori seaweed, crumbled (optional)
    1 egg yolk, beaten

Boil stock, add rice and ginger. Lower heat and simmer until rice is well cooked and starting to disintegrate (30 minutes for white rice, up to one hour for brown rice). Season with salt and black pepper. Add the peas, nori and beaten egg yolk. Simmer for further ten minutes and serve.

Miso Soups

The most convenient way of adding miso to a pan of hot soup or water is to make a creamy paste of the miso in a cupful of the hot liquid, then add the paste to the pan and stir. The sort of miso to use in the recipes is not stipulated, but where you have a choice, experiment with the different types and find the flavour that suits you most.

Tofu Miso Soup

    1 l (2 pt) clear soup stock or water
    1 small carrot, grated
    1 small onion, diced
    100 g (4 oz) miso
    175 g (6 oz) tofu, cut into 2.5 cm (1 in) squares
    1 pinch togarashi

Combine the stock, carrot and onions and bring to the boil, reduce heat and simmer for five minutes. Add the creamed miso, stir well, then drop in the tofu. Return to the boil. Turn off heat, add a pinch of togarashi, stir and serve.

Vegetable Miso Soup

   2 tablespoons vegetable oil
   50 g (2 oz) mushrooms, sliced
   100 g (4 oz) daikon or turnip, matchsticks
   1 small onion, diced
   100 g (4 oz) burdock root, peeled and grated (optional)
   100 g (4 oz) miso
   1 l (2 pt) clear soup stock or water
   2 tablespoons parsley, chopped or 1 sheet nori, crumbled

Place the oil in a heavy pan, and sauté the mushrooms, daikon, onion and burdock. When the onions are soft add the stock and bring to the boil. Cream the miso and stir into the soup. Return to the boil, and serve garnished with parsley or nori.

Chilled Summer Vegetable Miso Soup

   1 l (2 pt) vegetable soup stock, chilled
   75 g (3 oz) miso
   100 g (4 oz) cucumber, thinly sliced and chilled
   100 g (4 oz) tomatoes, diced and chilled
   Small bunch fresh mint, chopped

Blend the stock and miso together. Divide the vegetables between four bowls, pour on the soup and garnish with mint.

Pork and Watercress Miso Soup

 1 l (2 pt) water
 225 g (8 oz) lean pork, diced
 1 bunch watercress, chopped
 100 g (4 oz) miso
 25 g (1 oz) ginger root, grated
 1 small leek, chopped and minced

Add the diced pork to the water and bring to the boil. Reduce heat and simmer for ten minutes. Cream the miso and add to the stock, stir well. Add the watercress and return to the boil. Sprinkle with leeks and ginger and serve.

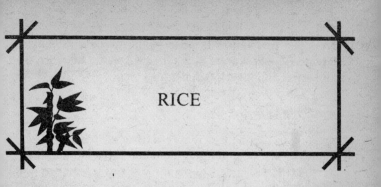

RICE

Inari, the rice goddess, is quite naturally held in high esteem by the Japanese farmer, and during the summer growing season she is courted assiduously. If she has behaved well, the farmer and his family are rewarded with a heavy autumn harvest as well as the back-breaking job of bringing it in. But afterwards, when the harvest is gathered, there will be traditional festivities and thanks to Inari over a cup of sake (or just as likely, nowadays, a glass of Johnny Walker whisky). The importance of rice to the farmer and the nation is reflected in the language, and although Japanese for rice is han, it is always given the highest honourable prefix and called go-han.

Most Japanese eat only white polished rice, not unrefined brown rice, just as we in the West eat mainly white bread. The trend towards eating polished rice began in the late fifteenth century, when Japanese aristocrats set the fashion, and it has slowly become standard practice for everyone. Nowadays, in Japan as elsewhere, there is a greater awareness of food values, and some younger people are starting to eat the more nutritious brown rice. But for older people brown rice is too attached in their minds to wartime rations, and the privations of that time, to start eating it now. Some of the following rice recipes can be easily adapted to brown rice, if you wish to use it, but others have been developed for, and taste better with, the lighter, fluffier, Japanese cooked white rice. The chapter on macrobiotic cookery contains recipes for brown rice.

Plain Boiled Rice

Short-grain Japanese rice is cooked until it is just sticky enough to pick up mouthful amounts with chopsticks. Other types of rice, with practice, can be cooked in the same way just as successfully. The amount of water used in cooking cannot be given precisely, since it depends on the rice used, but an approximate water to rice ratio is $1\frac{1}{2}$–$1\frac{3}{4}$ volumes of water for 1 volume of rice. After cooking rice a few times by the following method, you will be able to judge how much water to use. The recipe specifies a particular volume of water, but this is just for guidance.

Basic Cooking Methods

450 g (1 lb) rice
850 ml ($1\frac{1}{2}$ pt) water

Wash the rice well by stirring it vigorously in lots of water. Let the rice settle and carefully pour off all the milky residue. Repeat the process until the water remains almost clear. Drain and place the rice in a heavy bottomed pan with a good lid. Add the cooking water, cover the pan and bring to the boil quickly. Turn the heat right down and allow to simmer for 15 minutes (longer for brown rice). Finally, turn the heat off and allow the rice to stand for 5–10 minutes. Serve rice from the pot using a wooden spoon or rice paddle (samegi). No salt is added.

Please note rice cooked with soy sauce tends to burn easily and takes longer to cook. Thus, when soy sauce is added to the cooking water, the heat should be lower and the cooking time longer than when cooking ordinary rice.

Green Rice (Na-Meshi)

450 g (1 lb) dry rice, washed and drained
850 ml (1½ pt) water
225 g (8 oz) fresh spinach or chrysanthemum leaves or
    watercress
Salt to taste

Cook rice by the basic method. Meanwhile, boil the greens in
the smallest amount of water (i.e. 1 or 2 tablespoons).
Immediately the leaves soften, drain and cool in water.
Drain again and press out excess liquid. Cut into shreds, add
to freshly cooked rice, salt to taste and mix together. Serve.

Red Rice

This dish is usually made with a variety of rice, called mochi,
that is sweeter than the regular kind. It is known as Sekihan
when made with mochi, and is a great favourite for festive
occasions, especially Hina Matouri or Girls' Day. A red
colouring is given to the rice by cooking it with aduki beans.
Mochi rice is not readily available in the West, and the recipe
given here will be for ordinary rice. If you cannot obtain aduki
beans, use red or kidney beans instead.

Rice and aduki beans eaten together provide a rich protein
source as well as a colourful dish.

100 g (4 oz) aduki beans, soaked in water six hours or more
1 l (2 pt) water
450 g (1 lb) dry rice, washed and drained
1 teaspoon salt
2 tablespoons sesame seeds, toasted

Drain the soaked beans. Place in pot with water, bring to the
boil, reduce heat and simmer until cooked (about one and a
half hours). Drain and reserve liquid. Put rice in pot, add the

bean cooking liquid plus, if necessary, enough water to make the volume up to 850 ml (1½ pt). Cover and bring to the boil. Add beans, mix and continue to simmer until rice is cooked. Combine salt and toasted sesame seeds. Serve red rice hot or cold, garnished with sesame seed and salt mixture (this mixture is called 'gomashio').

Chicken with Rice

175 g (6 oz) boned chicken breast cut into 2.5 cm (1 in) cubes
25 g (1 oz) ginger root, grated
2 tablespoons sake or sweet wine or medium sherry
2 tablespoons soy sauce
1 tablespoon sugar
450 g (1 lb) dry rice, washed and drained
850 ml (1½ pt) chicken stock
225 g (8 oz) mushrooms, sliced
2 sheets nori, toasted *or*
1 tablespoon parsley, finely chopped

Marinate the chicken in the ginger, sake, soy sauce and sugar for 30 minutes or longer. Add the mushrooms, then gently boil the mixture until the chicken pieces are just tender. Place rice in heavy pan, add the chicken stock and any marinating liquid not absorbed by the chicken and mushrooms during cooking. Bring to the boil, stir in chicken and mushroom, reduce heat, cover pot and carefully simmer for 15 minutes. Turn off heat, allow to stand 15 minutes. Serve garnished with crumbled toasted nori or parsley.

Egg and Chicken Triangles on Rice

Part of the appeal of this dish is its colourful attractive presentation, and it is a good addition to a dinner party or buffet table.

450 g (1 lb) dry rice, washed and drained
850 ml (1½ pt) water
2 tablespoons soy sauce
450 g (1 lb) cooked chicken, diced
25 g (1 oz) ginger root, grated (optional)
2 tablespoons mirin or sweet sherry
1 tablespoon sugar
3 eggs, beaten
Pinch of salt
1 bunch parsley, chopped

Cook the rice by the basic method. While it is simmering put chicken in small heavy pan with soy sauce, ginger root and mirin or sherry. Gently boil for two or three minutes with constant stirring. Cover and simmer. Add pinch of salt to eggs and scramble. Lay a bed of rice in a shallow square or rectangular serving dish. Join two corners of the dish with a line (over the rice) of chopped parsley. Two triangles are formed, in one arrange the chicken and sauce, and in the other the scrambled eggs.

White Fish with Rice

450 g (1 lb) sole or halibut
1,425 ml (2½ pt) water
450 g (1 lb) dry rice, washed and drained
1 tablespoon vegetable oil
1 clove garlic, crushed
100 g (4 oz) mushrooms, sliced
4 spinach leaves, chopped
Pinch of salt
1 tablespoon soy sauce
1 tablespoon watercress or parsley, chopped
1 sheet nori, toasted (optional)

Cut the fish into three or four pieces, and boil in water until tender. Strain, reserve the liquid. Remove flesh from bones and shred into small pieces. Cook rice by basic method using 850 ml (1½ pt) of fish stock instead of water. Just before you set the rice to simmer, stir in the flaked fish and then proceed as normal. Lightly sauté garlic in pan with oil, then add mushrooms, spinach and pinch of salt. Cover, lower heat and simmer until mushrooms are soft. Now pour in the remaining fish stock and soy sauce, and heat to boiling. Place rice and fish mixture in individual bowls, pour over the mushroom and spinach broth, and garnish with watercress or parsley and sprinkle with toasted nori.

Deep Fried Rice Balls with Barbecue Sauce

Deep fried food seems to have universal appeal, and this rice ball dish is no exception. You may add other ingredients to the recipe than those suggested, e.g. minced beef, flaked fish, chopped vegetables, etc.

675 g (1½ lb) cooked rice
1 medium leek, finely chopped
2 tablespoons vegetable oil
2 tablespoons miso
2 cloves garlic, crushed
25 g (1 oz) ginger root, grated
50 g (2 oz) plain flour, sieved
Oil for deep frying (including, if possible, 25 per cent sesame seed oil)

BARBECUE SAUCE

100 ml (4 fl oz) soy sauce
100 ml (4 fl oz) mirin or sweet sherry
1 tablespoon sugar

Combine barbecue sauce ingredients and gently simmer uncovered, until reduced to half original volume. Meanwhile, thoroughly mix all the other ingredients except the flour. Lightly wet hands and shape mixture into small balls (2.5–5 cm (1–2 in) in diameter). Heat deep frying oil in wok or other pan, to about 175°C (350°F) or until you see a slight haze forming above the oil, roll rice balls in flour and deep fry (6–8 at a time) until brown and crisp. Drain well. If you are making a large quantity, keep the fried rice balls hot in a medium oven. Serve with barbecue sauce. Dip hot balls in sauce before eating.

Fried Rice

2 tablespoons vegetable oil
1 clove garlic, crushed
1 medium onion, diced
100 g (4 oz) mushrooms, sliced
100 g (4 oz) celery or French beans, chopped
450 g (1 lb) cooked rice
1 fresh egg or a 1-egg omelette, cut in strips
2 tablespoons soy sauce

Heat the oil in a heavy frying pan. Add the crushed garlic and onion. Sauté until onions are just soft, and then add the mushrooms and celery. Fry gently for two or three minutes retaining the texture of each vegetable. Stir in the rice. Heat through, stirring constantly. Break the egg over the rice mixture, sprinkle on the soy sauce and mix well. Serve. Alternatively, for a fried rice with a less creamy texture, replace the egg with strips of omelette.

Donburi

Donburi dishes are large bowls of rice or noodles combined with vegetables or meat, and served topped with egg and perhaps a sauce. Alternatively, the vegetables and meat are mixed with the egg and the whole is fried, before topping the rice. Donburi means 'big bowl'. They can be rich dishes filled with many ingredients or simply cooked rice combined with left-over vegetables topped with an omelette.

Chicken Donburi

For four to six people.

   1 small chicken or chicken pieces weighing 450 g–1 kg (1–2 lb)
   450 g (1 lb) dry rice, washed and drained
   850 ml (1½ pt) water
   225 ml (8 fl oz) reserved chicken stock
   2 tablespoons mirin or sweet sherry (optional)
   2 tablespoons soy sauce
   225 g (8 oz) mushrooms, sliced
   100 g (4 oz) peas (fresh, frozen or tinned)
   3 eggs, beaten
   1 teaspoon salt

Cut the chicken into four or five pieces and boil in the minimum of water until tender. Strain and reserve liquid. Remove the bones and skin from the chicken pieces and cut the flesh into small pieces. Cook rice by the basic method. Place part of the reserved chicken stock in a large pan and add the mirin or sherry, soy sauce, mushrooms and peas. Cook until vegetables are just soft. Gently mix into the pan the rice and chicken. Combine the egg and salt and pour over rice mixture. Stir well and maintain low heat until egg is just set. Serve in 'big bowl'.

Vegetable Donburi

  4 shiitake or 100 g (4 oz) mushrooms, sliced
  450 g (1 lb) dry rice, washed and drained
  2 tablespoons vegetable oil
  2 small leeks or 2 spring onions, thinly sliced
  1 medium carrot, grated
  4 leaves spinach, chopped
  2 sticks celery, chopped
  2 tablespoons soy sauce
  2 teaspoons sugar
  Salt to taste
  Pinch of togarashi or black pepper

Soak the shiitake for 20 minutes in cold water, remove any hard stems and thinly slice. Cook the rice by the basic method. Meanwhile, heat the oil in a heavy pan and sauté the vegetables and mushrooms until just soft. Add the soy sauce, sugar and salt to taste. Pour over the beaten eggs, add a pinch of togarashi, stir and cook until eggs just set. Put cooked rice in serving bowl, top with egg and vegetables and serve.

Tempura Donburi

Tendon, an abbreviation of tempura and donburi, is the name used for this dish, which is a bed of rice topped with tempura (fish or vegetables and meat dipped in batter and deep fried). Recipes for tempura are given in the chapter on tempura and fried foods (see p. 161)

Japanese Curried Rice

See Curried Noodles (p. 68)

SUSHI

Sushi is the word used to describe a variety of dishes in which cooked rice seasoned with vinegar and sugar is the basic ingredient. The sushi shop is very popular in Japan, where it is used as a casual bar where one can relax and sit down to a snack or meal and drink. Sushi is prepared with all sorts of ingredients in a variety of combinations. It serves the same purpose as, and can be compared to, the Western sandwich. A box of assorted sushi is convenient for lunchtimes, picnics or travelling, and they are sold from take-away booths at airports, stations, etc.

There are three main types of sushi. The simplest but somehow most difficult to make perfectly is nigiri-sushi. As with many processes, the simplest method requires the most skill if it is to be executed perfectly. The vinegared rice is moulded with wet hands into an oval, round, square, etc. shape and topped with a slice of fish, vegetable, egg or pickle. For sashimi or raw fish garnish, the rice patties are first dabbed with a little wasabi (green Japanese mustard). An alternative way of making nigiri-sushi is to mix the garnish and rice before shaping. The patty is then sprinkled with toasted nori or sesame seeds.

Norimaki-sushi is rice and other ingredients wrapped in a thin sheet of nori seaweed. The resulting Swiss roll shape is cut into thick slices and each piece displays the colourful filling.

The nori seaweed may be replaced by a thin egg omelette cut into a rectangular shape. Egg-wrapped sushi or yushiki-sushi as they are called, are an excellent replacement for norimaki-sushi if nori is not available.

Chira-sushi, our third category, is a sort of rice salad, in which various ingredients and sushi rice are mixed.

An assortment of various sushi served with thin slices of fresh ginger and soy sauce makes a fine meal.

Sushi Rice – Basic Method

The quantities given in this recipe may not be suitable for all types of rice, and you may need to experiment a little to find the exact combination of cooking water and sugar/vinegar mixture to give the best sushi rice. Do remember the success of the dish depends on the quality of the sushi rice. It should be tasty, sticky enough to mould, but not the least bit squashy or mashed up.

The quantities given for the sushi dressing will make enough for several preparations of sushi rice. Reserve what you do not use and store in the refrigerator.

Sushi Rice (for four people)

450 g (1 lb) dry rice, washed and drained
850 ml (1½ pt) water
2–3 tablespoons sushi dressing

SUSHI DRESSING

100 ml (4 fl oz) vinegar
175 g (6 oz) sugar
1 tablespoon salt

To prepare sushi dressing, combine vinegar, sugar and salt and bring to the boil. Turn off heat and leave. Use hot or cold; either way it gives the same result.

Cook the rice by the basic method for plain rice, then turn it into a wooden or non-metallic bowl. Pour dressing over the hot rice until a little remains unabsorbed in the bottom of the bowl. Now stir the rice gently with a wet rice paddle or wooden spoon, while the other hand fans the rice with a flat pan lid or rolled up newspaper. This cools the rice quickly and gives it an authentic shine.

Nigiri-Sushi

Prepare the sushi rice by the basic method (see above) and while it is still warm, prepare rice patties as follows. Wet your hands and using about one heaped tablespoon of rice, form a shape (e.g. oval, ball, square, etc.) in the palm of your hands. Continue until all the rice is used up. Wet your hands as necessary to prevent the rice sticking to them. Arrange the rice shapes on a serving dish and garnish with one or more of the suggested toppings below.

Garnishings for Nigiri-Sushi

Quantities have not been given, since the amount needed will depend on how much sushi rice you have prepared, and how many different toppings you want to use.

(1) Thin egg omelette cut into strips and brushed with soy sauce
(2) Fresh uncooked slices of sashimi (see p. 106), sparingly spread with wasabi or English mustard
(3) Smoked salmon in small pieces, sprinkled with fresh lemon juice
(4) Anchovies
(5) Cooked shrimps
(6) Sardines
(7) Prawns, shelled: leave tail intact and lightly cook
(8) Mussels, cooked

(9) Sliced pickled herring
(10) Fresh cucumber, sliced and sparingly spread with wasabi or English mustard
(11) Sliced mushrooms, lightly cooked in equal parts of soy sauce and sugar
(12) Cooked vegetables, cut into suitable shapes
(13) Cooked chicken or meat, thinly sliced
(14) Sesame seeds, toasted
(15) Fish paste: grind cooked fish and garlic in a suribachi or mortar and spread on sushi
(16) Nori seaweed, toasted and crumbled

Remember you may mix the garnishing with rice before moulding into shape. The filled sushi is then garnished with toasted nori or sesame seeds.

Norimaki-Sushi

Norimaki-sushi traditionally has six different fillings, but of course you may use as many as you wish. The fillings are prepared before the sushi is rolled in the seaweed wrapping. This is not a recipe that can be written out in a regular fashion, and for clarity I have divided it into two parts. The first describes how to assemble the norimaki, and the second gives a list of fillings. The amounts given for each filling will, in combination with three or four other components, make enough norimaki for four to six people. See page 53 for egg-wrapped sushi.

Assembly of Norimaku-Sushi

Sushi rice for four people (see p. 47)
Fillings (see below)
4 sheets of nori

Hold nori seaweed over a direct heat source to crispen it. Place on a bamboo screen or mat (called a sudare) approximately 20 cm × 20 cm (8 in × 8 in), or a damp cloth of the same size (this makes the wrapping process a little more difficult, but nothing insurmountable). Divide the rice into four portions and spread one portion over the sheet of nori, leaving a 2.5 cm (1 in) gap at the top and bottom ends to allow for overlap. Lay the fillings in horizontal rows down the middle of the rice. Slightly moisten the exposed edges of the nori and then roll up the mixture in the mat or cloth. Make sure the ingredients are tightly encased by the seaweed and then unroll carefully. Trim the ends and cut roll into 2.5 cm (1 in) thick slices. Repeat for each sheet of nori. See diagram.

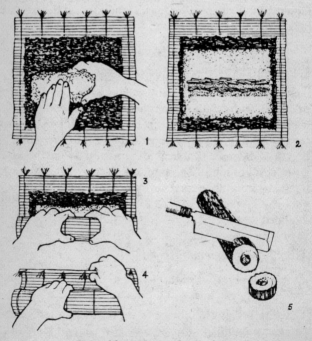

Assembling Norimaki-Sushi

Norimaki-Sushi Fillings

(1) CARROT

    1 medium carrot, quartered lengthwise and cut into sticks
       0.5 cm ($\frac{1}{4}$ in) thick

    1 tablespoon vegetable oil

    1 tablespoon water

    Pinch of salt

Sauté the carrot sticks in oil for two minutes. Add water and pinch of salt. Simmer until carrots are just soft.

(2) LOTUS ROOT

    1 medium lotus root, quartered lengthwise and cut into
       sticks 0.5 cm ($\frac{1}{4}$ in) thick

    1 tablespoon soy sauce

    1 tablespoon water

Combine ingredients and heat through.

(3) SPINACH

    100 g (4 oz) spinach

    2 tablespoons water

    Pinch of salt

    1 tablespoon sesame seeds, toasted

Boil spinach lightly in salted water for two to three minutes. Drain, chop and mix with sesame seeds.

(4) FRENCH BEANS

    100 g (4 oz) French beans

    Water to cover

    Pinch of salt

Cover beans in water, bring to the boil, add a pinch of salt. Simmer for three to four minutes. Drain and store in cold water.

(5) EGG

Beat 2 eggs. Prepare paper thin omelettes and cut into 0.5 cm (¼ in) wide strips

(6) FISH

50 g (2 oz) prawns, peeled and cooked *or* filleted salmon, halibut or plaice

2 eggs, beaten

1 tablespoon sake or white wine

Pinch of salt

2 tablespoons oil

Pound prawns or fish in suribachi or mortar, add beaten egg, sake and pinch of salt. Mix well. Heat oil in heavy frying pan, pour mixture in and quickly fry on both sides. Cut into thin strips.

(7) SHIITAKE OR MUSHROOMS

4 shiitake or 100 g (4 oz) mushrooms, thinly sliced

4 tablespoons water

½ tablespoon sugar

½ tablespoon soy sauce

Soak the shiitake for 20 minutes in cold water. Remove any hard stems and thinly slice. Omit this for fresh mushrooms. Cook mushrooms in remaining ingredients until soft.

(8) WATERCRESS

1 bunch watercress, chopped

(9) SASHIMI

100 g (4 oz) sashimi (see p. 106) cut into lengths 0.5 cm (¼ in) square

(10) CUCUMBER

½ medium cucumber, peeled and cut into long matchsticks

Wasabi or English mustard to taste

Sparingly dab cucumber strips with wasabi before laying in norimaki.

The above suggestions should be supplemented with your own ideas. Make full use of leftover cooked vegetables, fish, meat, etc.

Yushiki-Sushi
To make yushiki-sushi proceed in exactly the same way as for norimaki-sushi, but substitute paper-thin omelette sheets for the nori. The recipe given below for thin omelettes makes the equivalent of eight sheets of nori.

Paper-thin Omelettes

    4 eggs, beaten
    ½ teaspoon salt
    2 tablespoons vegetable oil

Add salt to beaten eggs, mix well. Coat a large, heavy frying pan with a little oil and heat well. Pour in one-eighth of the egg, tilt the pan to spread egg evenly and cook over medium heat. Turn omelette over when fairly hardened on bottom side. Cook both sides.

For norimaki cut the omelettes into squares approximately 20 cm × 20 cm (8 in × 8 in). Use trimmings for filling.

Chakin-Sushi
This recipe also makes use of egg-wrapped sushi, but utilizes a different shape wrappings to yushiki-sushi. Chakin-sushi consists of rice-filled egg pouches garnished with shrimps and green peas. See diagram overleaf.

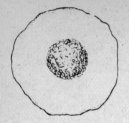

Assembling Chakin-Sushi

225 g (8 oz) sushi rice (see p. 47)
8 paper-thin omelettes (see p. 53)
100 g (4 oz) shrimps, cooked
50 g (2 oz) green peas, cooked
2 tablespoons parsley, chopped

Spread out a roughly circular paper-thin omelette and place
one-eighth of the sushi rice in the centre. Gather the edges of
the omelette together, and draw to the centre. Fold back the
edges, leaving an opening at the top. Tie the pouch into
shape by fastening coloured string or cotton under the folds.
Garnish the top of the rice in each pouch with shrimp, peas
and parsley.

Chira-Sushi

This vinegared rice salad, or 'Vinegared Rice with Fish and
Vegetable Mingled' as I've seen it described on a Japanese
menu, can be prepared with a multitude of ingredients.
Traditionally, it requires nine different garnishings, but you
may wish to use less. Again there is no absolutely specific
recipe, but I have given a fixed recipe as a guide, and
followed it with a list of alternative ingredients. If you add or
replace or subtract ingredients from the given recipe you will
need to adjust amounts accordingly. The recipe is authentic
but straightforward for the Western cook. If you wish to try

more exotic garnishings see the alternatives suggested at the end of the recipe. The quantities given will prepare chira-sushi for 4–6 people.

Sushi rice for 4 people (see p. 47)
3 tablespoons vegetable oil
1 medium carrot, finely diced
1 medium onion, finely diced
1 stick celery, finely chopped
50 g (2 oz) mushrooms, chopped
1 teaspoon sugar
2 teaspoons soy sauce
1 egg, beaten
50 g (2 oz) salmon, tinned or fresh boiled
50 g (2 oz) green peas, cooked
25 g (1 oz) ginger root, finely sliced
1 tablespoon sesame seeds, toasted
Salt to taste

Sauté the carrot, onion and celery in 2 tablespoons of oil until just soft. Combine the beaten egg with 1 teaspoon of soy sauce, a pinch of salt and prepare a pancake-thin omelette with the mixture, cut into strips. Cook mushrooms in 1 tablespoon of oil, stir in sugar and remaining soy sauce. Flake the salmon and season with salt. Gently mix the sushi rice with cooked vegetables, strips of omelette and salmon. Transfer the mixture to serving bowl, heaping it to a point in the middle. Garnish the top with green peas, slivers of ginger root, and sprinkle with sesame seeds. Serve hot or cold.

ALTERNATIVE INGREDIENTS FOR CHIRA-SUSHI
  (1) 50 g (2 oz) filleted white fish (halibut, cod, plaice, hake, etc.), fried and flaked
  (2) 50 g (2 oz) shrimps (fresh or tinned). If you use fresh shrimps leave shell on and boil in a little water. Remove shell and soak shrimps in vinegar before use.

(3) 50 g (2 oz) sashimi (see p. 106)

(4) 50 g (2 oz) anchovies

(5) 50 g (2 oz) mussels (raw or poached)

(6) 50 g (2 oz) pickled herring, sliced

(7) 50 g (2 oz) sardines

(8) 4 shiitake. Soak in cold water for 20 minutes, remove
    any hard stems and slice

(9) 100 g (4 oz) tofu cut into 2.5 cm (1 in) cubes

(10) 50 g (2 oz) French beans, lightly boiled in salted water

(11) 50 g (2 oz) bamboo shoots, thinly sliced or cut in half
     moon shapes

(12) 50 g (2 oz) lotus root, thinly sliced, quartered

(13) 75 g (3 oz) chestnuts, cooked, peeled and chopped

(14) 50 g (2 oz) fresh bean sprouts.

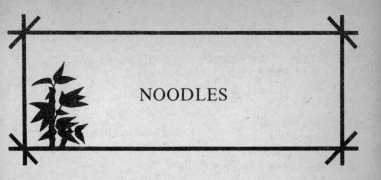

NOODLES

Italy is usually most associated with pasta dishes, but in the shape of noodles pasta has been eaten in the Far East for thousands of years. Noodles, one of Japan's most basic foodstuffs, lend themselves to a wide range of dishes and methods of preparation. Noodles in steaming hot soup topped with chicken, pork or vegetables, stir fried with vegetables, served alone with a simple dipping sauce or garnishing, or in the summer chilled in a salad or mixed with cold sautéed vegetables, are a few of the 'oodles of noodles' dishes.

Udon, somen and soba are the three main types of Japanese noodles. Udon and somen are made from wheat flour, and they are related in the way spaghetti is to vermicelli (two suitable substitutes respectively). That is, udon is a fat noodle and somen a thin one. Soba are buckwheat flour noodles; they tend to be a little chewier and tastier than the wheat flour variety, and are perhaps the Japanese' favourite noodle. They are often eaten on festive occasions and especially at New Year to ensure a happy and lucky year ahead, the length of the noodle representing longevity and continuity.

It is not difficult to make your own noodles, and recipes are given for preparing udon and soba. Otherwise, packets of both these noodles and somen are available in health/

wholefood stores. Alternatively, other types of pasta can be used.

Traditionally in the East, flour has been used to prepare noodles – not to make bread. Flour in noodle form is easily digestible, and noodles made with some or all wholewheat or buckwheat flour are nutritious as well as delicious.

The chapter is arranged in the following order: preparation and cooking of noodles, noodles in soup stock, dipping sauces and garnishings for noodle dishes, fried noodles and finally other hot noodle dishes. Where a recipe specifies just noodles either udon, somen or soba may be used. Soup stock is called for in a number of recipes; if you do not have any available, bouillon cubes are a good substitute.

Preparation and Cooking of Home-made Noodles
One pound of noodles serves five to six people.

Udon (Wheat flour noodles)

100 g (4 oz) wholewheat flour and 350 g (12 oz) strong,
   plain white flour
or 450 g (1 lb) plain white flour
1 teaspoon salt
150 ml (5 fl oz) water, approximately

Mix flour and salt in a large bowl, then gradually add water to form a slightly dry dough. Knead for 10 to 15 minutes. Flour a board and roll out dough into a thin (approximately 0.25 cm [$\frac{1}{8}$ in] thick) rectangular sheet. Fold the two narrow ends of the sheet into the middle, fold again at the middle to divide dough into quarters. See diagram on page 59.

With a sharp knife, cut folded sheet crosswise into 0.25 cm ($\frac{1}{8}$ in) strips. Unroll noodles and spread on floured board to await cooking.

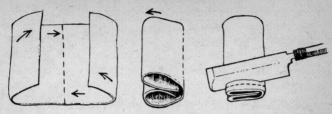

Boil 2 l (4 pt) water, carefully lower in noodles and return water to boil. Add 225 ml (8 fl oz) cold water and bring to the boil a second time. Reduce heat and simmer until noodles are cooked but still just hard at the core (approximately 10 minutes). This method of cooking ensures that both the inside and outside of the noodles are evenly cooked. Drain noodles and rinse under cold running water separating any noodles that are stuck together. To reheat pour boiling water over the noodles. Note, the water in which the noodles were cooked may be reserved and used for preparing soup stock.

Soba (Buckwheat Flour Noodles)

450 g (1 lb) buckwheat flour
1 teaspoon salt
1 egg, beaten
100 ml (4 fl oz) water, approximately

Place the flour and salt in a large mixing bowl, thoroughly mix, add beaten egg and stir in. Gradually add water to form a slightly dry dough. Proceed as for udon noodles on previous page.

To cook Dried Noodles

For four people:

    350 g (12 oz) dried noodles
    3 l (5 pt) water

Either follow instructions on the packet or use following
method. Bring water to the boil, add noodles and stir gently.
Return to the boil, reduce heat until water is just bubbling.
Cook uncovered until noodles are cooked, but still just hard
at the core (approximately five minutes). Drain, and if not to
be used immediately, rinse under cold running water. Stand
to drain well. Use as required. If storing add a little soft
butter or oil to stop the noodles sticking together. To reheat,
pour boiling water over noodles.

Noodles in Soup Stock

Simple Udon or Soba
This is a basic method. For more elaborate and more filling
udon or soba, try some of the toppings suggested below.

    350 g (12 oz) udon or soba, cooked and drained
    1 l (2 pt) hot soup stock
    2 tablespoons chives or spring onions, chopped and/or
        other garnishings (see below)
    Soy sauce to taste

Divide noodles among four bowls, pour over soup stock and
garnish with chives or spring onions.

Other possible toppings are: parboiled carrot slices;
bamboo shoots or lotus root slices, cooked; fresh or frozen
garden peas or other vegetables; slices of mushroom or
soaked shiitake sautéed in oil; pieces of cooked chicken or
pork; whole shrimp; hard boiled egg slices; abalone slices.

Also see garnishings suggested for Noodles with Egg and Vegetables (below) and Soba Noodles with Dipping Sauce (p. 62).

Noodles with Egg and Vegetables

This is a basic recipe. For a more elaborate dish, see suggestions below.

   350 g (12 oz) udon, parboiled and drained
   1 l (2 pt) soup stock or water
   100 ml (4 fl oz) soy sauce
   4 tablespoons mirin or sweet sherry
   1 tablespoon sugar
   50 g (2 oz) small mushrooms, whole
   2 small leeks, cut into 5 cm (2 in) pieces
   4 eggs
   2 tablespoons parsley, minced
   Togarashi or black pepper to taste

Place parboiled noodles in large casserole, bring stock or water, soy sauce, mirrin and sugar to the boil and pour over noodles. Arrange mushrooms and leeks on top and carefully break in four eggs, separately. Cover and bring to the boil. Reduce heat and simmer until eggs are cooked. Serve garnished with parsley and togarashi to taste. Below are suggested alternatives and/or additions to ingredients in the recipe. They should be added before the eggs.

(1) 100 g (4 oz) cooked chicken, cut into small pieces
(2) 4 shiitake, soaked in cold water for 20 minutes.
   Remove hard stems, criss-cross the tops with sharp knife. Cook in 2 tablespoons sugar and 2 tablespoons soy sauce until liquid is absorbed.
(3) 225 g (8 oz) French beans, parboiled in salted water 3 to 4 minutes, drained

(4) 1 medium carrot, thinly sliced, parboiled in salted
water 3 to 4 minutes, drained
(5) 4 stalks spinach or chrysanthemum leaves, parboiled
in a little salted water, drained, chopped in 2.5 cm (1 in)
lengths.

Five Colour Noodles (Gomokusoman)

4 shiitake or 100 g (4 oz) mushrooms
2 tablespoons sugar
2 tablespoons soy sauce
2 eggs
100 g (4 oz) French beans, parboiled in a little salted water
1 tablespoon vegetable oil
1 green pepper, de-seeded, cut into 1.25 cm (½ in) strips
½ medium cucumber, thinly sliced
100 g (4 oz) cooked ham, thinly sliced
350 g (12 oz) somen, cooked and drained

Soak shiitake in cold water 20 minutes. Remove hard stems,
criss-cross the tops with a sharp knife. Cook shiitake or
mushrooms in sugar and soy sauce until the liquid is
absorbed. Prepare four paper-thin omelettes (see p. 53) and
cut into narrow strips. Heat oil in a heavy pan and lightly
sauté green pepper. Heat noodles by pouring boiling water
over them. Drain and distribute noodles among four bowls.
Decorate the top of the noodles with the five prepared
ingredients and serve.

Noodles with Dipping Sauces and Garnishings

Soba Noodles with Dipping Sauce

This is a dish in which the noodles are cooked, topped with a
wide range of garnishings and served either with a separate
dipping sauce or with the sauce poured over. A basic recipe is
given with three different dipping sauces. Additions and

alternatives to the recipe follow. This dish can also be made
with udon, but it is not quite as tasty as with soba.

   350 g (12 oz) soba, cooked and drained
   4 tablespoons leeks, chives or spring onions, finely
     chopped

SAUCE I
   75 ml (3 fl oz) vinegar
   100 ml (4 fl oz) soup stock
   2 tablespoons sugar

SAUCE II
   100 ml (4 fl oz) soy sauce
   100 ml (4 fl oz) mirin or sweet sherry
   225 ml (8 fl oz) soup stock
   Pinch of togarashi or black pepper

SAUCE III
   4 tablespoons soy sauce
   2 tablespoons mirin or sweet sherry
   350 ml (12 fl oz) soup stock
   2 tablespoons miso
   2 tablespoons sesame seeds, toasted and pounded to paste
     in suribachi or mortar

Combine ingredients of whichever sauce you choose to
make, and bring to the boil. Place soba on one large plate or
bowl. Divide sauce among four bowls and garnish each with
leeks, etc. Dip noodles into sauce before eating. Both
noodles and sauce can also be served cold. The other way to
serve the dish is to divide the noodles among four bowls,
pour over the sauce and garnish.

ALTERNATIVE GARNISHINGS
  (1) The garnishings suggested for Simple Udon or Soba
      (see p. 60) and Noodles with Egg and Vegetables (see
      pp. 61–2)
  (2) 2 paper-thin omelettes (see p. 53), cooled, cut into strips
  (3) ½ medium cucumber, peeled, cut into half lengthwise
      and thinly sliced. Marinate in 1 tablespoon vinegar and
      1 tablespoon sugar before using
  (4) 2 tablespoons sesame seeds, toasted
  (5) 2 sheets nori, toasted and crumbled

Keep garnishes separate when arranging on top of noodles.

Noodles Cooked with Miso

This is equally delicious hot or cold. If you obtain Cha soba
(green noodles made with green tea powder) they go
particularly well with the miso sauce. Spinach-based pasta is
an effective substitute.

    2 tablespoons miso
    575 ml (1 pt) soup stock
    2 tablespoons mirin or sherry or white wine
    1 tablespoon sugar
    2 tablespoons soy sauce
    2 tablespoons sesame seeds, toasted (optional)
    2 tablespoons vegetable oil
    1 medium onion, thinly sliced
    50 g (5 oz) mushrooms, thinly sliced
    25 g (1 oz) ginger root, grated
    350 g (12 oz) noodles, cooked and drained

Cream the miso with a little stock, then combine first seven
ingredients, mix well and bring to the boil. Sauté onion,
mushrooms and ginger in oil in heavy pan. Stir in the miso
mixture and noodles and bring to the boil. Reduce heat and
simmer for 10 minutes. Serve hot or cold.

Fried Noodles

There are two ways of frying noodles: soft fried in a little oil
or deep fried. Udon, somen and soba can be fried by either
method. In each case the noodles are pre-cooked, drained
and cooled. To soft fry noodles, heat 2 to 3 tablespoons oil,
in a heavy frying pan. Add 225 g (8 oz) cooked noodles and
sauté with constant stirring for 4 to 5 minutes. To deep fry,
separate the cooked noodles into single strands, fill heavy
pan or deep frying pan with 7-10 cm (3 to 4 in) oil and heat to
175°C (350°F). Drop in the noodles, a handful at a time, and
fry until medium brown in colour. Remove with chopsticks
and drain on absorbent paper.

Soft Fried Udon or Soba

This is a basic recipe; more elaborate additions are suggested
below.

4 tablespoons vegetable oil
1 clove garlic, minced
25 g (1 oz) of ginger root, grated (optional)
½ medium carrot, grated
100 g (4 oz) Chinese cabbage, chopped
1 medium green pepper, diced
350 g (12 oz) udon or soba, cooked and drained
Togarashi or black pepper to taste
Soy sauce to taste

Heat the oil in a heavy frying pan, sauté the garlic and ginger
for 2 to 3 minutes, then add the other vegetables. Fry until
just soft cooked. Stir in the noodles, heat through, season
with soy sauce and togarashi. Other ingredients that can be
fried with noodles are:

(1) 2 paper-thin omelettes (see p. 53), cut into 2.5 cm
(1 in) strips
(2) 100 g (4 oz) French beans, cut into 2.5 cm (1 in) pieces

(3) 2 stalks celery, chopped
(4) 1 medium onion, diced
(5) 2 spring onions, chopped
(6) 100 g (4 oz) bean sprouts
(7) 100 g (4 oz) cooked meat, sliced
(8) 100 g (4 oz) cooked fish, whole or sliced
(9) 1 medium lotus, sliced, or bamboo shoots
(10) 50 g (2 oz) mushrooms, sliced
(11) 4 shiitake, soaked for 20 minutes, hard stems removed, sliced
(12) 175 g (6 oz) tofu, 2.5 cm (1 in) cubes
(13) 175 g (6 oz) fried tofu, cut into 1.25 cm (½ in) cubes
(14) 100 g (4 oz) cheese, grated
(15) 100 g (4 oz) beans (soya, aduki, kidney, etc.) cooked. Combine with 2 tablespoons soy sauce, separate beans into equal portions, mash one portion, salt, recombine
(16) 100 g (4 oz) shrimps or prawns, shelled, deveined and cooked (see p. 105) or tinned

Fried Soba with Spinach

This is not as far as I know, a traditional Japanese recipe, but I was given it by an American friend living in Japan. It looks Japanese, but tastes a little too much of garlic to be really authentic. My friend's mother was Italian. Anyway it's delicious.

2 tablespoons oil
4 cloves garlic, crushed
450 g (1 lb) fresh spinach, washed, coarsely chopped and drained
350 g (12 oz) noodles, cooked
Salt and black pepper to taste

Heat the oil in a heavy pan. Add the garlic and sauté until light brown (about 3 minutes). Drop in the spinach, cover pan and lower heat. Stir occasionally. Simmer until spinach is completely wilted. Now stir in noodles, season with salt and black pepper and heat through. Serve.

Fried Soba with Eggs

   3 tablespoons vegetable oil
   4 eggs, beaten
   Pinch of salt and black pepper
   175 g (6 oz) Chinese cabbage, chopped
   1 medium onion, thinly sliced
   3 tablespoons soy sauce *or* 2 tablespoons miso
   350 g (12 oz) soba, cooked and drained

Coat a heavy pan or frying pan with 1 tablespoon oil, heat and pour in the eggs. Season with salt and black pepper and scramble until well cooked. Remove eggs from pan and reserve. Add remaining oil to pan and lightly sauté cabbage and onion for about 3 minutes. Stir in the soy sauce or miso, mix well, add noodles and scrambled eggs and heat through. Serve.

Deep Fried Noodles (Yaki Soba)

Yaki soba was the first dish I learned to order in Japanese. The name rolls off the tongue and the pronunciation is easy, but that is not the only reason for asking for it. The Japanese are masters at deep frying and yaki soba allows this talent full expression.

   2 tablespoons vegetable oil
   ½ medium carrot, cut into matchsticks
   1 medium onion, cut into thin wedges
   1 green pepper, cut into 1.25 cm (½ in) strips
   50 g (2 oz) mushrooms, sliced

2 tablespoons cornflour (blended with 4 tablespoons water)
1 tablespoon soy sauce
Oil for deep frying
225 g (8 oz) noodles, cooked and drained

Heat oil in a heavy pan, add all the vegetables and sauté for 4 to 5 minutes. Add water until the vegetables are just covered, cover pan, simmer for 5 minutes, then stir in cornflour and soy sauce and simmer a further 5 minutes. Deep fry noodles according to method given (see p. 65), drain on absorbent paper and divide among four bowls. Pour over vegetable sauce and serve.

Other Hot Noodle Dishes

Curried Noodles

The ubiquitous curry has even reached Japan although in a much milder version than the Indian variety. It is popular served over noodles or rice. Modern youngsters eat curry with a spoon rather than chopsticks, and I remember sitting in a café near Okinawa University eating a bowl of soba, feeling proud because of my deftness with the chopsticks, when all around me sat students shovelling down curry and rice with spoons!

2 tablespoons vegetable oil
225 g (8 oz) chicken, lean pork or beef, diced into small cubes
1 medium onion, thinly sliced
2 medium potatoes, diced
1 medium carrot, thinly sliced
100 ml (4 fl oz) water
1–2 teaspoons mild curry powder
Pinch of salt

350 g (12 oz) noodles, cooked and drained
25 g (1 oz) ginger root (grated), chutney *or*
  2 tablespoons finely chopped spring onion

Brown the meat or chicken in oil in a heavy pan, add the
vegetables and sauté until soft. Make a paste with a little of
the water and curry powder and add it with remaining water
to pan. Add salt and ginger and cook while stirring for 5 to
10 minutes. The consistency should be quite thick; simmer to
reduce liquid if necessary. Either stir in the noodles and
warm through or heat noodles by pouring boiling water
over them and serve curry sauce over the noodles. Garnish
with chutney or, more authentically, with chopped spring
onions.

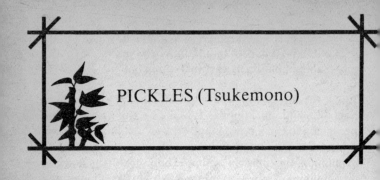

PICKLES (Tsukemono)

For many foreigners, more than anything else, the distinctive and appetizing smell of pickled vegetables or tsukemono reminds them of Japanese market places and households. Every sort of vegetable is pickled, although the most popular are Chinese cabbage and daikon. The pickles have a slightly crisp texture and tangy flavour, a good contrast to the blandness of white rice, and the two are often eaten together as a lunchtime snack.

A variety of pickling agents are used, including neat miso, but the most common are salt or a rice bran and salt mixture. Rice bran is the brown skin that surrounds each grain of rice and which is removed to give white rice. The vegetables to be pickled are left whole or cut into suitable shapes, layered in a wooden tub with lots of salt and pressed down with a heavy weight. The longer they are pressed, the more they come to resemble pickles. After four or five days the vegetables will have lost much of their water content and be submerged in a brine solution. The pickles are removed as required, rinsed in plenty of water, chopped up and served in small amounts with soy sauce and grated ginger. For a crispier and longer-lasting pickle, the vegetables are air dried before pickling. Daikon, particularly, is pickled in this way when it is known as 'all winter long' takuan. This salt-pressing pickling process is easily applied in a Western kitchen, and it is a useful way of preserving surplus garden vegetables.

Tsukemono and other pickled vegetables

In all the salt-pressing techniques the vegetables will continue to ferment in the tub for as long as you leave them. Thus when they become as sour as you wish, drain off the liquid and either store the pickles in a container in the refrigerator or bottle them in air-tight jars.

The quantities given in recipes that require vinegar are for malt or wine vinegar. The Japanese use a mild rice vinegar and if you use this type, increase the volume of vinegar stipulated in the recipes by one and a half times.

Salt-Pressed Pickle or Salad – A General Method

Whether salt-pressed vegetables are called pickles or salads depends upon the duration of the pressing time. Many vegetables are delicious prepared this way, and, particularly in winter, they are more satisfying than a regular cold salad. Try cabbage, turnip, carrot or onion to start with.

Cut root vegetables into matchsticks or slices and chop or shred green vegetables into fine pieces. Place the vegetables in a large wooden tub, bowl or non-metallic container and generously sprinkle with salt. Place a wooden lid or plate directly on top of the vegetables and weigh down with water-filled pan, stone, etc. Leave for one hour to five days. Pour off excess liquid as it collects or leave for more sour pickles. Use pickles as required and rinse in cold water if too salty. A small amount of pickles accompanying another dish is the best way to eat these salt-pressed vegetables.

Mixed Vegetable Tsukemono

4 medium carrots, thinly sliced
2 small turnips, quartered and sliced
1 small cabbage, cut in strips
2 cucumbers, thinly sliced
450 g (1 lb) French beans (leave whole)
Salt
4 to 5 small chilli peppers (optional)

Place vegetables in colourful layers in a wooden tub or earthenware container. Generously sprinkle each layer with salt. Place a wooden lid or plate (about 1 kg [2 lb]) directly on top of the vegetables and weigh down. Leave to ferment for four to five days, then use as required. Serve with soy sauce and/or vinegar or sesame seed oil. To prepare hot pickles, distribute the chilli peppers in the layers of vegetables before adding the salt. Soak the pickles in cold water if too salty for your taste.

Any of the vegetables used in the recipe can be prepared in the same way singly or in any convenient combination. Other suggestions are lettuce, daikon, spinach, cauliflower or aubergine.

An alternative method of salt pickling is as follows. Sterilize a number of large preserving jars and carefully load the vegetables in a colourful neat pattern. Boil a solution of salt and water (500 ml [1 pt] water to 450 g [1 lb] salt), cool and pour over vegetables. Cover and leave for a week. Remove pickles with fork or chopsticks, sterilized in boiling water.

Various Pickling Recipes

Quick Pickle

These pickles are ready two to 24 hours after preparation.

2 small turnips, quartered and diced
2 medium carrots, matchsticks
4 cabbage leaves, finely chopped
Peel of 1 lemon, grated
2 tablespoons salt

Sprinkle the cabbage leaves with a little of the salt, allow to stand for five minutes, then squeeze out the excess liquid by gently pressing. Mix all the ingredients in a salad bowl. Place a wooden lid or plate 675 g (1½ lb) directly on the top of the vegetables and weigh down for two to 24 hours. Store unused pickle in the refrigerator.

Daikon or Turnip Tsukemono

This is another quick method of preparing fresh daikon or turnip pickles.

900 g (2 lb) daikon or small white turnip
Salt
225 g (8 oz) sugar
100 ml (4 fl oz) vinegar

Wash the vegetables and slice crosswise into neat 0.15 cm (⅛ in) thick circles. Place in colander and sprinkle with salt, ensuring it is evenly distributed throughout. Leave for one hour, then rinse and squeeze dry in a clean cloth. Transfer to a storage jar and pour over vinegar and sugar. Stir well. Refrigerate and use as required.

Vinegar-pressed Vegetables

450 g (1 lb) vegetables (see next page)
275 ml (10 fl oz) vinegar
2 tablespoons sugar
2 teaspoons salt
4 tablespoons sesame seeds, toasted and crushed (optional)

Suggested vegetables – alone or in combination:

Carrots, thinly sliced
Cabbage, finely shredded
Cucumber, thinly sliced
Red or green pepper, deseeded, cut into 2.5 cm (1 in) strips
Aubergine, sliced, salted, rinsed and drained

Combine vinegar, sugar and salt, and bring to the boil. Add the crushed sesame seeds and cool. Place vegetables in salad bowl or other non-metallic container with wide mouth, and pour on vinegar mixture. Stir well, then place a wooden lid or plate (about 1 kg [2 lb]) directly on top of vegetables and weigh down. Leave two to three hours. The vegetables can now be served. Leave whatever is not used in the pickling liquid and store in the refrigerator.

Pickled Mushrooms

This is not a pickle in the sense that it can be preserved over a long period. It does, however, keep well in the refrigerator. Serve hot or cold.

450 g (1 lb) mushrooms, whole, halved or quartered (depending on size)
4 spring onions, finely chopped
175 g (6 oz) sugar
225 ml (8 fl oz) soy sauce
Salt to taste

Bring the sugar and soy sauce to the boil. Add the spring onions and simmer for two minutes. Toss in the mushrooms and return to the boil. Boil for three minutes, remove from the heat and allow to stand for ten minutes. Drain off the liquid, reserve for further use. Serve mushrooms hot or cold.

Sweet and Sour Pickled Cucumbers

> 4 medium cucumbers, washed and thinly sliced
> Salt
> 100 ml (4 fl oz) vinegar
> 2 tablespoons soy sauce
> 175 g (6 oz) sugar

Salt cucumber and place in a colander. Cover with plate plus weight, and press for 30 minutes. Rinse and squeeze dry in clean cloth. Combine other ingredients and stir until sugar is dissolved. Transfer cucumber to jar and pour over sweet and sour dressing. Chill and serve. Store unused pickle in a refrigerator.

Pickled Melon

Once when I visited a friend's house in Japan, his father invited me to taste his home-made wine. It turned out to be a jar full of garlic cloves covered with sake, sealed and left for a year or two. I had a small glass. The taste is hard to describe, but I can still remember it. Fortunately, pickled melon has a much different taste, even though it uses the same pickling agent.

> 1 small melon, peeled, seeded and cut into 2.5 cm (1 in) cubes
> 275 ml (½ pt) sake or medium sherry
> 2 tablespoons brandy
> Pinch of salt

Put melon cubes into a sterilized preserving jar. Add the other ingredients, seal and leave for at least three days. Serve as a dessert. You may need to add more sake and brandy if the amount given does not cover the melon.

Pickled Aubergine Salad

1 large aubergine
Salt
3 tablespoons soy sauce
3 tablespoons sugar
3 tablespoons mirin or sweet sherry
1 teaspoon dry English mustard

Quarter the aubergine and cut each quarter into thin slices. Sprinkle salt generously over slices and lay in colander to drain. Leave 30 minutes to soften, rinse thoroughly, press out excess moisture and pat dry on a clean cloth. Prepare a thin paste of the other ingredients and coat aubergine with it. Cover and chill for two hours before serving.

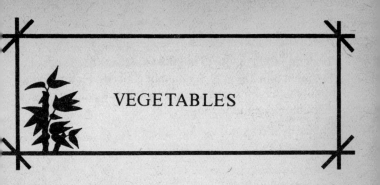

VEGETABLES

For general information on Japanese cooked vegetables, see the Introduction. The vegetable recipes have been arranged in alphabetical order, with the first letter of a vegetable's best-known English name deciding its position. The methods used in the preparation of vegetable dishes are designed to retain and highlight the individual taste, texture and colour of each vegetable. Recipes containing vegetable ingredients are to be found in nearly every chapter in the book but in this chapter, with one or two exceptions, the recipes will be solely vegetable dishes.

Aubergines (Egg Plant)

Japanese aubergines are smaller and a little tenderer than the Western variety, but the two are interchangeable. Before cooking aubergines should be sliced, or cut into whatever shape is required for the recipe, placed in a colander, sprinkled with salt and left for 30 minutes to an hour, then rinsed and drained. This process removes excess moisture and bitter juices. Aubergines are not normally peeled before use. Remember that aubergine dishes often improve when reheated and are usually as good cold or hot.

Grilled Aubergine

This is an excellent way to prepare aubergines for people on a low-fat diet. In Japan they would be cooked over a charcoal fire; if you have a barbecue grill try it this way, otherwise a preheated oven grill will do.

    450 g (1 lb) aubergines, cut into 2.5 cm (1 in) thick slices,
        salted, rinsed and drained
    Salt
    Soy sauce to taste

Preheat grill. Dry aubergines on a clean cloth. Very lightly sprinkle with salt. Grill until soft (two to three minutes each side). Serve with soy sauce.

Spicy Aubergines (Korai Nasubi)

    450 g (1 lb) aubergines, cut into 2 cm (¾ in) cubes, salted,
        rinsed and drained
    4 tablespoons oil
    25 g (1 oz) ginger root, grated
    1 clove garlic, crushed
    Good pinch 7-spices pepper or cayenne or hot pepper
        sauce
    1 medium leek or onion, thinly sliced
    75 ml (3 fl oz) soup stock or water
    1 teaspoon sugar
    1 tablespoon chopped chives or parsley or spring onion *or* 1
        sheet nori, toasted, crumbled

Heat oil in a heavy pan, add aubergines and sauté for three to four minutes. Stir frequently. Remove aubergines from the pan, drain and reserve excess oil. Put aubergines to one side and return reserved oil to pan. Add ginger, garlic, leek, and 7-spices pepper and sauté over high flame for 30 seconds. Reduce heat, pour in stock and sugar and mix well. Add the aubergines, bring to the boil. Turn off heat and serve garnished with chives, etc.

Beef-Stuffed Aubergines

2 large or 4 small aubergines
Salt
175 g (6 oz) minced beef
1 egg
50 g (2 oz) breadcrumbs
½ medium onion, diced
2 teaspoons soy sauce
Pinch salt and togarashi or black pepper
2 tablespoons sesame seeds, toasted
2 to 3 tablespoons cornflour
Oil for deep frying
50 g (2 oz) ginger root, grated

Cut aubergines lengthwise down the middle, but do not cut completely in half; leave about 2.5 cm (1 in) of stem end intact. Soak in lightly salted water. Meanwhile, combine beef, egg, breadcrumbs, onion, soy sauce, salt and pepper and mix well. Drain aubergines, pat dry on clean cloth and open them out as much as possible. Sprinkle cornflour on inside surfaces and stuff beef mixture between. At this point it may be necessary to clamp edges together with toothpicks. Sprinkle bulging edges of stuffing with any remaining cornflour. Pour oil 7.5–10 cm (3–4 in) deep into a heavy pan, heat to 175°–180°C (350°–360°F), or until you see a haze forming above the oil and carefully lower in stuffed aubergines. Deep fry four to five minutes. Remove with slotted spoon and serve with grated ginger. Minced pork or chicken or shrimps may be used in place of beef.

Bamboo Shoots (Takenoko)
Even tinned bamboo shoots retain the crunchy texture of the

fresh plant, and they contrast well with softer vegetables if the two are served together.

Boiled Bamboo Shoots

225 g (8 oz) bamboo shoots, cut into 1.25 cm ($\frac{1}{2}$ in) thick matchsticks
450 ml (1 pt) soup stock
2 teaspoons soy sauce
1 tablespoon sugar

Combine all the ingredients in a heavy pan. Bring to the boil, reduce heat and simmer for approximately 15 minutes. Drain, reserve liquid for further use if required. Serve.

Grilled Bamboo Shoots

2 tablespoons soy sauce
1 tablespoon vinegar
1 tablespoon sake or white wine or dry sherry
1 teaspoon sugar
Pinch 7-spices pepper or cayenne
2 tablespoons soup stock or water
225 g (8 oz) bamboo shoots cut into 0.5 cm ($\frac{1}{4}$ in) thick slices

Combine first six ingredients and bring to the boil. Remove from heat, add bamboo shoots and marinate for one hour. Drain and reserve liquid. Grill bamboo shoot slices under low flame for five to six minutes each side. Brush each side two to three times with marinade liquid during grilling.

Bean Sprouts (Moyashi)

More often used in conjunction with other vegetables or fresh in salads, bean sprouts are nevertheless tasty just quick fried with garlic and ginger. They are normally grown from mung beans. For a plant food they have a very high protein to calorie content ratio.

Fried Bean Sprouts

2 tablespoons vegetable oil
1 clove garlic, crushed
2 tablespoons soy sauce
25 g (1 oz) ginger root, grated
450 g (1 lb) bean sprouts
Togarashi or black pepper to taste

Heat oil in a heavy pan, add garlic and sauté for two to three minutes. Add soy sauce, ginger and bean sprouts. Toss about in pan and fry until bean sprouts have softened but not completely wilted (about three minutes). Serve sprinkled with togarashi or black pepper.

Bean Sprouts with Tofu

Bean sprouts and tofu combined are a rich source of vegetable protein.

2 tablespoons oil
1 clove garlic, crushed
1 medium onion, diced
350 g (12 oz) tofu, cut in 2.5 cm (1 in) cubes
350 g (12 oz) bean sprouts
1 teaspoon salt
1 tablespoon soy sauce

Heat oil in a heavy pan, add garlic, sauté for two to three minutes. Add onion and tofu. Fry, stirring constantly, until tofu is lightly browned on both sides. Add bean sprouts, salt and soy sauce. Mix well, heat through and serve very hot.

Broccoli

This hardy vegetable thrives well in colder, mountainous areas, of which there are many in northern Japan. Substitute cauliflower, cut into small flowerettes or Brussels sprouts, left whole if small, otherwise halved, for broccoli in any of the following recipes.

Broccoli with Soy Sauce and Sesame Seeds

    2 l (3 pt) water
    1 teaspoon salt
    450 g (1 lb) broccoli, cut into flowerettes
    2 tablespoons sesame seeds, toasted
    2 tablespoons soy sauce

Cook broccoli as described in recipe below. Serve sprinkled with sesame seeds.

Broccoli with Mustard Sauce

    2 l (3 pt) water
    1 teaspoon salt
    450 g (1 lb) broccoli, cut into flowerettes
    2 tablespoons dry English mustard
    2 tablespoons water
    2 tablespoons soy sauce
    2 tablespoons sugar

Bring water to boil, add salt and parboil broccoli for three to four minutes. Drain. Combine other ingredients, pour over broccoli and leave to marinate for one hour. Serve cold or drain off marinade, heat to boiling, toss in broccoli, heat through and serve.

Burdock (Gobo)

Burdock is a dark brown root vegetable, long, thin, and tapering to a point at one end. In Japanese markets they are sold in bunches or at stalls that specialize in burdock and they can be bought in bags, already peeled, soaked and chopped. This work is all done by hand, in between serving the customers and is fascinating to watch. Unfortunately, burdock is no longer generally available in the West (although more available in America than Europe) but in Japan it is an important and widely used vegetable. It has a tough texture, and the larger ones are sometimes pounded with a heavy wooden roller before use. To prepare burdock for cooking, hold the root under running water and scrape off the dark peel. Cut into 5 cm (2 in) long pieces and cut these individually into thin matchsticks. Alternatively, thinly slice into rounds. Soak burdock pieces in cold water for 20 minutes to remove slightly alkaline taste. Drain, cover with water and simmer until tender.

Cabbage (Chinese and White)

Chinese cabbage either pickled, quick fried, or in soups, salads or stuffed is most popular in Japan. It is now generally available in the West, but if you have any trouble obtaining it, ordinary white cabbage is a good substitute. Chinese cabbage takes a slightly shorter time to cook than white cabbage, so in the recipes allow a slightly longer cooking time for the latter. The recipes, unless otherwise stated, are good for both types of cabbage.

Plain Braised Cabbage

  450 g (1 lb) cabbage, coarsely chopped
  2 tablespoons vegetable oil
  Soy sauce and togarashi or black pepper to taste

Heat oil in a heavy pan, add cabbage and sauté briskly over a high heat. Stir frequently. After two to three minutes, reduce heat, cover and simmer for 10 to 15 minutes. Stir occasionally. Serve seasoned with soy sauce and togarashi to taste. To add colour to the dish, add one medium carrot, cut into matchsticks, to cabbage before cooking.

Cabbage Rolls

    8 large cabbage leaves
    4 shiitake or 100 g (4 oz) mushrooms
    2 tablespoons vegetable oil
    1 medium onion, finely diced
    ½ medium carrot, grated
    4 tablespoons soy sauce
    1 teaspoon salt
    1 teaspoon sugar
    50 g (2 oz) cooked somen or vermicelli cut into 5 cm (2 in)
      lengths
    450 ml (1 pt) soup stock *or* 450 ml (1 pt) water and 5 cm (2
      in) piece of kombu
    2 tablespoons parsley

Place cabbage leaves in a colander and pour boiling water over them. Reserve water and repeat process with the same water until the leaves just soften up. Put aside. Soak the shiitake in cold water for 20 minutes. Drain, cut away any hard stems and thinly slice. Alternatively, use thinly sliced mushrooms. Heat oil in a heavy frying pan, add onion and fry until light brown, drop in carrots, then mushrooms. Stir fry each one for two minutes after addition. Add noodles, 2 tablespoons soy sauce, ½ teaspoon salt and sugar, mix well and remove from heat.

Lay one cabbage leaf flat and, on one end, spoon 2–3 tablespoons of sautéed vegetables and noodles. Roll the leaf up, tucking in the ends and secure with a toothpick or twine. Repeat for each leaf. Put stock or kombu and water in pan, add remaining soy sauce and salt and bring to the boil, lower in cabbage rolls, return to the boil, reduce heat, cover and simmer for ten minutes. Lift rolls out with slotted spoon, arrange in serving dish, pour over some of the cooking liquid, garnish with parsley and serve. For variety add minced meat or chicken to the stuffing mixture.

Chinese Cabbage and Spinach Rolls

This is a good method of serving greens. Even children enjoy the colour and taste.

    8 Chinese cabbage leaves
    225 g (8 oz) spinach
    Salt
    2 tablespoons soy sauce
    1 tablespoon lemon juice

Place cabbage leaves in a colander and pour boiling water over them. Reserve water and repeat process with same water until leaves just soften up. Pour over cold water and set aside. Collect the stems of the spinach leaves together and tie spinach into four bunches with twine. Cook bunches in a little salted water until stems are just soft. Drain, rinse in cold water. Place two cabbage leaves flat and overlapping. Remove twine from one bunch of spinach and lay the spinach horizontally across cabbage leaves. Roll into a tight bundle and squeeze out excess moisture. Repeat with remaining ingredients and allow rolls to stand for 20 minutes. Cut into 2.5 cm (1 in) thick sections. Serve sprinkled with soy sauce and lemon juice. Replace spinach with watercress if it is more easily available or for variation.

Carrots
Did you ever as a child turn your nose up at boiled cabbage

or spinach? Well, Japanese children seem to reserve this reaction for the poor carrot, but don't let that put you off the recipes.

Carrots with Sesame

    2 tablespoons vegetable oil
    2 medium carrots, grated
    Salt to taste
    2 tablespoons sesame seeds, toasted

Heat the oil in a heavy pan, add the carrots and sauté for five minutes. Stir frequently. Season with salt to taste, stir in the sesame seeds, sauté for a further five minutes and serve.

Boiled Carrots

As for Boiled Bamboo Shoots (see p. 80), but substitute 2 medium carrots, cut into flower shapes, for the bamboo shoots.

Celery

Celery is a rarity in Japan, and is considered a special treat. It is cooked very lightly.

    100 ml (4 fl oz) water
    4 stalks celery, cut on the bias into thin slices
    Salt

Bring to the boil, add salt, drop in celery and cook over high heat for one minute. Drain. Serve with either of these sauces:

SESAME SEED SAUCE

    3 tablespoons sesame seeds
    1 tablespoon soy sauce
    2 tablespoons water

Grind sesame seeds to a paste in suribachi or mortar. Stir in soy sauce and water. Mix well. Pour over celery.

SOY AND GINGER SAUCE

    3 tablespoons soy sauce
    1 teaspoon sugar
    50 g (2 oz) ginger root, grated

Combine and pour over celery.

Corn on the Cob
A regular sight during the summer in the southern islands of Japan are roadside vendors selling corn on the cob grilled over an open charcoal fire. Served very hot and a touch blackened, they are handed to the buyer with a toothpick stuck in either end. A lovely snack and excellent barbecue meal. To barbecue simply coat corn with oil and cook over charcoal fire, rotating regularly to ensure even cooking. Serve with soy sauce or butter if you wish.

    More conventionally you may cook corn on the cob in the oven. Preheat oven to 230°C (450°F). Wrap corn in aluminium foil and bake for 10–15 minutes.

Cucumber
The Japanese do not normally cook cucumber, but rather serve it chilled with other vegetables and a dressing (see Pickles p. 70).

French Beans
Young French beans topped and tailed parboiled in a little salted water for four to five minutes, drained, immersed for a few moments in cold water, to preserve their colour, and served on their own make an excellent side dish. French beans are also used in many Japanese recipes as a garnishing or as an ingredient in pickles or cold cooked salads.

Japanese Radish (Daikon)

The name means large root, and these vegetables can indeed be up to 60 cm (two feet) in length and 30 cm (1 foot) in circumference. They have quite a sharp flavour when fresh and grated. Fresh daikon is used to add bite to a dish either as a garnish or in a dipping sauce. Cooked or salted the flavour becomes milder. Small white turnips make a good substitute. With young daikon the greens can be cooked in a little salted water and served with soy sauce. They are a rich source of Vitamin C.

Daikon is not generally available in the West, except at specialist shops, but it is worth trying to obtain if you know a stockist. Substitute daikon in any of the turnip recipes (see pp. 97–9) also see Pickles (p. 70).

Leeks

The flavour of the Japanese leek is milder than the Western variety, and more akin to the taste of young leeks. Both the green stem and white root section are used. Thinly sliced leek is particularly popular as a garnishing in clear soups or dipping sauces. Scallions or spring onions or young leeks can be used in any of the recipes that specify leeks.

Grilled Leeks

    4 leeks, sliced into 3.75 cm (1½ in) lengths
    2 tablespoons vegetable oil
    2 tablespoons miso
    2 tablespoons sugar
    2 tablespoons mirin or sherry (optional)
    OR
    4 tablespoons soy sauce
    Pinch of 7-spices pepper or cayenne

Pre-heat grill. Divide leek pieces on to four skewers. Brush with oil. Combine miso, sugar and mirin or soy sauce and 7-

spices pepper. Grill leeks until lightly browned all over. Remove from the grill and brush with either miso or soy sauce mixture. Return to the grill and cook a further two minutes. The sauce-brushed leeks will burn easily so take care. Serve hot.

Skewered Vegetables

This follows the same method and uses the same brushing sauces as for Grilled Leeks (above), but utilizes a variety of vegetables.

    1 leek, sliced into 3.75 cm (1½ in) lengths
    100 g (4 oz) tofu cut into four pieces, deep fried (see p. 100)
    1 small carrot cut into four pieces, parboiled in lightly
        salted water for four to five minutes
    1 small lotus root, cut into four pieces

Pre-heat grill. Skewer vegetables in a colourful pattern on each of four skewers. Now follow exactly the same method as for Grilled Leeks, using the same basting sauces.

Lotus Root (Renkon)

The fresh variety is not generally available, but tinned lotus root retains the slightly sweet flavour and slightly crunchy texture of the fresh vegetable. The hollow spaces that run its length form lovely patterns when it's sliced, and lotus root adds to the visual impact of any cooked or salad dish to which it is added.

Lotus Root and Lemon

    225 g (8 oz) lotus root, thinly sliced
    2 tablespoons vegetable oil
    Juice of 1 lemon
    2 tablespoons water
    Pinch of salt

Heat oil in a heavy pan, add lotus root and gently sauté on both sides for two to three minutes. Squeeze in lemon juice, water and pinch of salt, cover and simmer for five minutes. Serve.

Marrow and Pumpkin

Kabocha are Japanese pumpkins. They are small with a green bumpy skin, and very cheap and popular in the autumn when they are harvested. The flesh is similar in colour and taste to the English marrow or American pumpkin, either of which makes a good substitute.

Boiled Marrow or Pumpkin

675 g (1½ lb) marrow or pumpkin, peeled, de-seeded, cut into 2.5 cm (1 in) cubes

STOCK I

2 tablespoons sake or white wine
2 tablespoons sugar
2 tablespoons soy sauce
450 ml (1 pt) soup stock or water

STOCK II

3 tablespoons soy sauce
2 tablespoons sugar
1 teaspoon salt
450 ml (1 pt) soup stock or water

Bring the ingredients of Stock I or Stock II to the boil, add the marrow or pumpkin, return to the boil, cover, reduce, heat and simmer until tender (10–15 minutes). Drain and serve hot with or without cooking liquid. For a more elaborate dish, top boiled marrow or pumpkin with cooked shrimps.

Mushrooms

There are a number of cultivated tree mushrooms unique to Japanese cookery, but only shiitake in dried form are generally available in the West. Shiitake are not cheap but worth the expense for a special treat. Otherwise substitute large fresh mushrooms.

Shiitake Simmered in Soy Sauce

    12 shiitake or 100 g (4 oz) large mushrooms
    350 ml (12 fl oz) water
    2 tablespoons sugar
    3 tablespoons vegetable oil (sesame is best)

Soak shiitake in water for 20 minutes. Drain and reserve the liquid. Cut away any hard stems and gently squeeze excess moisture from shiitake back into soaking liquid. Criss-cross the caps with light knife cuts. Heat 2 tablespoons oil in a heavy pan, add shiitake and sauté over a high heat until they are browned. Add remaining ingredients and soaking liquid and simmer over low heat until all liquid has been absorbed or evaporated and the shiitake looks shiny (about 30 minutes). Serve hot or cold.

Alternatively, use 100 g (4 oz) large fresh mushrooms, miss out soaking section and substitute 175 ml (6 oz) water for soaking liquid where it is added to sautéed mushrooms.

Grilled Shiitake or Mushrooms

    8 shiitake or 225 g (8 oz) large mushrooms
    3 tablespoons soy sauce
    3 tablespoons mirin or sweet sherry
    Pinch 7-spices pepper or cayenne

Soak shiitake in water for 20 minutes. Drain, reserve liquid for soup stock. Cut away any hard stems. Combine soy sauce and mirin and marinate shiitake or mushrooms in mixture for one hour. Drain, reserve liquid. Grill shiitake or mushrooms lightly, top side up, for two to three minutes, and brush with marinade twice. Turn over and repeat. Serve sprinkled with 7-spices pepper or cayenne. This dish goes well with turnip or daikon pickle (see p. 73).

Onions

Onion with Sesame Seed

    2 tablespoons vegetable oil
    2 medium onions, cut into thin wedges or crescents
    1 teaspoon salt
    2 tablespoons sesame seeds, toasted

Heat the oil in a heavy frying pan, add the onions and fry until lightly brown, reduce heat, season with salt and gently cook a further ten minutes. Serve sprinkled with sesame seeds.

Onions and French Beans in Spiced Sauce

    2 tablespoons vegetable oil
    1 clove garlic, crushed
    2 medium onions, thinly sliced
    100 g (4 oz) French beans, parboiled in lightly salted water
    1 tablespoon miso
    100 ml (4 fl oz) soup stock or water
    $\frac{1}{2}$ teaspoon 7-spices pepper or hot pepper sauce
    1 tablespoon cornflour

Heat oil in a heavy pan, add the garlic, sauté for one minute, add the onions, sauté until lightly browned. Stir in the beans and gently heat. Cream miso in a little of the stock or water and add the remaining liquid and 7-spices pepper or hot pepper sauce to pot. Cream cornflour in 2 tablespoons of

liquid from the pot and stir in. Simmer, stirring constantly
until sauce is thickened and creamy. Serve as a side dish or
over rice or noodles.

Chrysanthemum Onions

Serve this unusual and exotic-looking onion preparation as
an accompaniment to a main meal.

    4 medium-sized onions
    450 ml (1 pt) soup stock or water
    1 teaspoon salt
    1 medium carrot, grated
    2 tablespoons sesame seeds, toasted *or* 2 tablespoons
        Miso and Mustard Dressing (see p. 98)
    1 tablespoon parsley, chopped

Quarter the onions, but do not cut right through. Leave the
root end intact. Place in pot, pour in stock or water, season
with salt and bring to the boil. Gently boil until onions are
cooked (about 15 minutes). Lift out onions and transfer to
four small bowls. Spread onions open and fill each with
grated carrot. Sprinkle with sesame seeds or Miso and
Mustard Dressing and garnish with parsley.

Peas

Fresh garden peas served on their own in individual bowls
with a sweet or savoury dressing is the favourite Japanese
way of serving them.

Sweet Peas

    350 ml (12 fl oz) water
    450 g (1 lb) fresh peas
    Pinch of salt
    50 g (2 oz) sugar
    1 teaspoon cornflour (optional)

Bring water to the boil, add peas and pinch of salt. Return to the boil, reduce heat and simmer until peas are just tender. Stir in the sugar, and for a thicker sauce add cornflour, creamed before addition in a little of the cooking liquid. Simmer very gently for a further 15 minutes. Serve.

Savoury Peas

350 ml (12 fl oz) soup stock
450 g (1 lb) fresh peas
Pinch of salt
1 tablespoon soy sauce
1 tablespoon sake or white wine
1 teaspoon cornflour (optional)

Repeat procedure for Sweet Peas, but replace water by soup stock, and sugar by soy sauce and sake.

Green Peppers

Sautéed Green Peppers

4 medium green peppers
2 tablespoons vegetable oil
2 tablespoons soy sauce
1 teaspoon sugar

Cut peppers into sixths, remove seeds and membranes. Heat oil over high heat, add peppers, soy sauce and sugar. Stir continuously and cook until peppers are just crisp. Serve.

Grilled Green Peppers

4 medium green peppers
2 tablespoons vegetable oil

Pre-heat grill. Quarter peppers, remove seeds and membranes. Brush with oil and grill for four to five minutes. Turn three to four times during grilling. Do not overcook; the peppers should remain semi-crisp.

Potato

Not as common as in the West, but widely used and available, due to some extent to the increase of hamburger cafés in Tokyo.

Potatoes with Miso

2 tablespoons vegetable oil
450 g (1 lb) potatoes, peeled, thinlyliced and cut into half
    or quarter moons
100 ml (4 fl oz) water
2 tablespoons miso
Salt and togarashi or black pepper to taste
2 tablespoons chives, chopped

Heat the oil in a heavy frying pan, add potatoes and sauté, frequently stirring, for five minutes. Pour in water, cover and simmer a further five minutes. Cream miso with a little cooking liquid and stir into pan. Simmer uncovered until most of the liquid has been absorbed or evaporated. Season and garnish with chopped chives.

Sweet and Sour Potatoes

50 g (2 oz) sugar
2 tablespoons vinegar
1 teaspoon salt
175 ml (6 fl oz) water
450 g (1 lb) potatoes, peeled, cut into 1.25 cm (½ in) cubes

Combine first four ingredients and bring to the boil. Add potatoes, return to the boil, cover, reduce heat and simmer until potatoes are cooked (about 15 minutes).

Seasoned Rice with Potatoes

This is a popular Okinawan country dish.

> 225 g (8 oz) rice, washed
> 100 g (4 oz) lean pork, thinly sliced
> 900 ml (2 pt) soup stock or water
> 450 g (1 lb) potatoes, peeled, sliced and cut into half moons
> 2 tablespoons miso
> 1 young leek or 2 spring onions, finely chopped
> 2 tablespoons vegetable oil (preferably sesame seed)

Place rice, pork and stock in a heavy pan, bring to the boil and add potatoes. Return to the boil. Cover, reduce heat and simmer for 30–40 minutes. Cream the miso with a little liquid from the pot and stir into the rice and potatoes. Remove pan from the heat and allow to stand for ten minutes. Stir in leeks, sprinkle oil over surface of food and serve.

Spinach (Horenso)

The Japanese tend to use young spinach leaves, and they normally leave the stems on. Steaming is the cooking method most favoured, since it retains the fresh green look of the young spinach. Chrysanthemum leaves (shungiku) are sometimes used where in the West we would use spinach. Shungiku is more fragrant and easier to overcook than spinach, but otherwise interchangeable. If you use shungiku in recipes that specify spinach, add one third more in weight than the amount of spinach required.

Steamed Spinach

> 450 g (1 lb) young spinach leaves
> Soy sauce and vinegar to taste

Lay spinach in steam basket, cover and steam for three to four minutes. Remove with chopsticks, cut into 2.5 cm (1 in) lengths and sprinkle with soy sauce and vinegar. Serve.

Alternatively, boil spinach in very small amount of water (1.25 cm ($\frac{1}{2}$ in)) in a heavy pan for three to four minutes. Continue as for steamed spinach.

Spinach with Sauce

Prepare 450 g (1 lb) cooked spinach as above and dress with one of the following sauces:

MISO AND EGG SAUCE

> 1 tablespoon miso
> 1 hard boiled egg, mashed
> 4 tablespoons stock or water
> Pinch 7-spices pepper or cayenne

Combine into a smooth paste. Mix with spinach.

LEMON SAUCE

> 3 tablespoons soy sauce
> 1 tablespoon sugar
> Juice of 1 lemon
> Pinch of salt

Combine and pour over spinach.

Turnips
Japanese turnips are small and mild in flavour. Substitute small white turnips.

Boiled Turnips

    4 small tender turnips
    450 ml (1 pt) soup stock *or* 450 ml (1 pt) water plus
        4 tablespoons sugar
    Soy sauce to taste

Quarter turnips to just over half their depth. Boil stock or water and sugar and turnips until tender (10–15 minutes). Drain, serve sprinkled with soy sauce. Alternatively, if stock is used, retain after draining and thicken up with a little cornflour (2 teaspoons), add soy sauce to taste and pour over turnips.

Turnip with Miso and Mustard Sauce

Prepare boiled turnips as described above, and dress with following sauce:

    3 tablespoons miso
    3 tablespoons vinegar
    3 tablespoons sugar
    1 tablespoon dry English mustard

Combine and mix well.

Chrysanthemum Turnips

Turn the poor plain turnip into a flower!

    2 small turnips
    Salt
    3 tablespoons vinegar
    1 tablespoon sugar
    1 red bell pepper, minced *or* peel of 1 lemon, grated
    Chrysanthemum leaves or lettuce

Cut stems off turnips and very finely peel. Stand on stem end and place a chopstick on each side of turnip. Now cut as though you were cutting whole turnip into slices but stop each stroke as knife meets chopsticks. Repeat across the other way to give a pine needle effect. Soak turnips in salted water until softened (30 minutes to 1 hour). Rinse, wipe dry on clean cloth, and stand in individual bowls. Combine vinegar, sugar and pinch of salt and pour over turnips. Allow to stand for three to four hours. Decorate by topping with small circles cut out of red pepper for red-centred, or lemon peel for yellow-centred chrysanthemums. Stand in bed of chrysanthemum or lettuce leaves to give flower effect.

Tofu

Tofu is made commercially by finely grinding dry soya beans, then cooking the coarse flour in water. The milky liquid formed is drained off and treated with a controlled amount of calcium sulphate which congeals it into a soft milky substance. This is poured into moulds and further drained through a fine cloth. The congealed solid is now lightly pressed and finally cut into small blocks for selling. Tofu is stored in cold water. It will keep for several days if the water is changed daily.

If you cannot find a source of buying fresh tofu, experiment with the following recipe until you can satisfactorily make your own.

450 g (1 lb) soya beans
3 tablespoons fresh lemon juice

Cover the soya beans with water and leave to soak for at least 12 hours. Change water once during soaking. Drain and grind the beans either in an electric grinder or hand mill. Transfer to a heavy pot and add 2½ times as much water by volume as beans. Bring to the boil, reduce heat and simmer for one hour. Arrange three to four layers of cheesecloth inside a colander placed over a large pan. Strain the contents of the pan through this. Finally, gather the cheesecloth around the collected pulp and squeeze out as much liquid into the pan as possible. Transfer the liquid to a glass bowl. Use the pulp in soups and stews. Add lemon juice to the liquid, stir once, cover with a damp cloth and leave in a warm spot (27°C [80°F] is perfect) for 8–12 hours or until tofu sets. Drain through cheesecloth to remove excess liquid. The tofu may now be used. For a professional look, pour it into a square mould, put a light weight on top and press for four hours. Store under water in a refrigerator.

For flavoured tofu, simmer a block of it or small squares in oil and soy sauce with mint, garlic, nutmeg, cinnamon, cloves, fennel or black pepper, or whatever seasoning you wish.

Deep Fried Tofu (Aburage)

Deep fried tofu or aburage is regularly used in casseroles and other dishes where long cooking would cause fresh tofu to disintegrate. The amount of fresh tofu given in this recipe yields 225 g (8 oz) of aburage.

  500 g (18 oz) or 3 blocks tofu
  Oil for deep frying

Before deep frying tofu, it must first be pressed to remove excess moisture. Slice the tofu blocks in half crosswise to give two thin slices each (six slices in total). Place the slices between two absorbent towels and place a cutting board or other weight on top. Leave for 30 minutes and then proceed to deep fry.

Pour enough oil into a heavy-bottomed pan or frying pan to come 2.5–3.75 cm (1 in–1½ in) up the sides. Heat pan on a high heat until a small piece of tofu dropped into the fat immediately bubbles (150°–175°C, 300°–350°F). Reduce heat slightly and carefully drop in half the tofu slices. Deep fry for one or two minutes or until tofu floats to the surface of the oil. Turn slices over and fry another two minutes. Lift from oil and drain on a rack for several minutes before using.

Mixed Vegetables and Tofu

Tofu is an excellent ingredient in mixed vegetable dishes. It absorbs the flavours of other ingredients and links them together. This recipe is for 6–8 people.

> 2 tablespoons vegetable oil
> 1 clove garlic, crushed
> 1 medium onion, thinly sliced
> 100 g (4 oz) cabbage, coarsely chopped
> 100 g (4 oz) broccoli, cut into flowerettes and/or 100 g
>   (4 oz) sprouts, quartered
> 1 small aubergine, salted, rinsed and drained
> 2 stalks celery, cut in 1.25 cm (½ in) lengths
> 100 g (4 oz) French beans, cut in 2.5 cm (1 in) lengths
> 1 medium green pepper, 2.5 cm (1 in) strips
> 1 bamboo shoot, sliced into half moons
> 1 lotus root, sliced into half moons
> 50 g (2 oz) mushrooms, sliced
> 1 teaspoon salt
> 1 teaspoon togarashi or black pepper
> 2 tablespoons soy sauce
> 275 ml (10 fl oz) soup stock or water
> 175 g (6 oz) tofu, cut into 2.5 cm (1 in) cubes and deep fried
>   (see previous page)
> 2 tablespoons mirin or sherry (optional)

Heat oil in an 'oven-to-table' type casserole, add garlic and sauté for one minute, add onions and lightly brown. Add all the remaining vegetables and stir fry for three to four minutes. Add remaining ingredients except tofu and mirin and bring to the boil, reduce heat and simmer for ten minutes. Drop in tofu and simmer for a further ten minutes. Finally pour in mirin or sherry and serve from casserole.

This recipe can be altered to include or exclude whichever vegetables are available or otherwise.

Oden

Oden is a popular winter casserole, often prepared for festive occasions when people can help themselves out of the oden pot, which can bubble away all evening without spoiling. In some big cities, they have vendors in the streets selling oden. From experience I can tell you they are not keen on customers who want to pick and choose from the oden pot. They believe in pot luck. The recipe is for 6–8 people.

   1 l (2 pt) soup stock
   1 teaspoon salt
   1 tablespoon sugar
   1 tablespoon soy sauce
   225 g (8 oz) daikon or small turnip cut into 2.5 cm (1 in) cubes
   1 medium carrot, cut into 5 cm (2 in) lengths
   1 kamaboko (a white fish cake, see p. 196) thickly sliced (optional)
   450 g (1 lb) tofu, deep fried (see p. 100)
   8 leaves cabbage, coarsely chopped
   3 bamboo shoots, cut in half, crosswise
   6 small potatoes
   6 hard boiled eggs

Combine the first four ingredients in a large pot and bring to the boil. Add daikon, carrot and kamaboko. Cook for 30 minutes, uncovered. Replenish evaporated liquid with soup stock or water. Add all the other ingredients and simmer slowly for 30 minutes. Invite each guest to ladle out some cooking liquid and a selection of vegetables, tofu, etc.

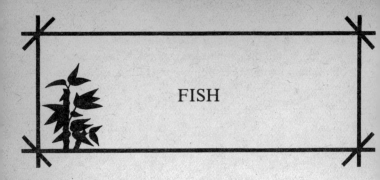

FISH

For a general discussion on fish see p. 2.

Buy fresh fish if you can, or, as second best, buy frozen fish. Look for shiny skin, bright eyes and firm flesh. Reject fish with any smell of staleness. Do not overcook. The inside flesh should remain moist, and it will just come away from the bones when the fish is perfectly cooked.

To clean round fish, work from tail to head, and scrape scales off both sides. Make a 5 cm (2 in) slit in belly below pectoral fin, and remove entrails, clean off scales and entrails cavity under cold running water. For flat fish remove gills, cut off fins, slice belly, remove entrails and wash under cold running water. Alternatively, ask your fishmonger to clean the fish and similarly if you require it filleted. Always ask for the bones, head, tail, etc., and then use them for preparing fish stock.

For grilled fish, the most popular Japanese cooking method, great care is taken to retain the shape of the fish during cooking. This is accomplished by 'stitching' the fish with skewers. A skewer is inserted near the eye of the fish and threaded along its length by bending the skewer up towards the top of the fins and then down again to the centre. Do not pierce the skin of the fish. Bring the skewer out of the tail end on an upward movement. This causes the tail to stand up when cooked. Insert a second skewer near mouth and repeat

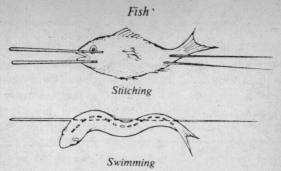

Stitching

Swimming

process, bringing this skewer out below the tail. For
'swimming' fish, push a skewer completely through fish at a
point just below the head. Force it back through to the other
side near the centre of the body and finally out again near the
tail. See diagrams.

To prepare prawns or shrimps for cooking, wash well,
remove shells, but in order to give a natural look, leave
tails intact, and, if you wish to devein, make a shallow cut
down the back of the shellfish and remove the vein (or
intestine tract) with a pointed knife or toothpick. To keep
shrimps straight during cooking, insert a toothpick between
the shell and flesh, starting at the head end and emerging at
the tail end.

The Japanese use five main methods to cook fish: grilling,
frying, baking, boiling and steaming. Then there is sashimi
or uncooked fish. The chapter is arranged by cooking
method, starting with sashimi.

Please note that in the recipes a particular type of fish is
not always specified. Instead a category of fish such as white
or red (oily) flesh is recommended. This is because the price
and availability of fish are always fluctuating, and it is often
wiser in terms of freshness and price not to have a fixed
shopping list. The recipes can be used to suit the type of fish
that is best value at any particular time.

Sashimi (see p. 2)

Take an absolutely fresh fish, remove skin and bones, cut the finest of the fillets into thin slices or cubes, serve in an attractive arrangement with garnishings, and there you have sashimi. A simple process but for some reason surrounded by mystique.

For the Western cook the most suitable fish for sashimi are salmon, tuna, seabream, halibut and red or grey mullet, although sole, smelt, trout and turbot are almost as good. Shellfish such as shrimps, prawns and lobster are also served in sashimi dishes. Ideally, they should be killed immediately before use and rinsed under cold water until firm.

Initially, it may be wiser to ask your fishmonger to prepare the filleted fish steak for you, but give him precise instructions. It should be as fresh as possible, free of all bones, and have no smell of fish. To cut white fleshed fish steak for serving, chill first and then cut, holding the knife at an angle of about 30°, into slices 1.25 cm ($\frac{1}{2}$ in) thick and 3.75 cm ($1\frac{1}{2}$ in) wide. Traditionally, the cuts are made from right to left, and the slices laid on top of another to the right. For red (oily) fish, cut straight down pulling the knife towards you, into pieces 1.25 cm ($\frac{1}{2}$ in) thick and 5 cm (2 in) wide. (Do not cut in a sawing fashion.) For small fish such as smelt or trout, shave off thin symmetrical slices of fish. To keep sashimi fresh, handle the fish as little as possible.

The sashimi is arranged in a dish in overlapping pieces and decorated with fresh raw vegetable garnishing. More than one type of fish may be used. Each person is given a small dish of soy sauce and one containing wasabi (Japanese mustard). The wasabi is mixed into soy sauce to taste and the pieces of sashimi are dipped into the mixture before eating. English mustard or horseradish sauce may be used in place of wasabi.

To Prepare Sashimi

450 g (1 lb) fresh filleted salmon steak (or tuna, halibut,
  seabream, red or grey mullet, etc.) *or*
4 large fresh prawns, cut into 3 pieces *or*
225 g (8 oz) fresh shrimps *or*
A combination of the above

GARNISHING

100 g (4 oz) cabbage, thinly shredded
1 medium carrot, shredded
½ bunch watercress
4 sprigs parsley

ADDITIONAL OR ALTERNATIVE GARNISHINGS

½ medium cucumber, shredded
½ bunch radishes, cut in shapes
2 small leeks, finely sliced
2 spring onions, finely sliced
100 g (4 oz) daikon, shredded

DIPPING SAUCE

1 tablespoon wasabi powder
1 tablespoon water
2 tablespoons soy sauce per guest
or
1 tablespoon English mustard powder
3 teaspoons water
2 tablespoons soy sauce per guest
or
2 tablespoons prepared horseradish sauce
2 tablespoons soy sauce per guest

Prepare and slice fish or shellfish according to the notes
given above. Chill until ready for use. Combine cabbage and
carrot and store in iced water until ready for use. Blend
wasabi or English mustard and water into a smooth paste or

use prepared horseradish sauce. In individual bowls arrange a layer of sashimi slices in a neat regular row (traditionally there are an uneven number of slices) or make a small mound of shellfish. Add a pinch of shredded carrot and cabbage, a few leaves of watercress and a sprig of parsley to each bowl. Serve with dishes of wasabi and soy sauce.

Alternatively, the sashimi can be arranged on one large serving dish and surrounded with garnishings. Each guest is given separate bowls of wasabi and soy sauce and helps him/ herself to sashimi from the central dish.

Grilled Fish

Yakimono, or grilled things, are traditionally cooked over a charcoal brazier or hibachi, and these recipes are excellent for barbecue-style cooking. However, they can be as equally well cooked and with less chance of things going wrong under a gas or electric grill. There are two characteristically Japanese methods of preparing the fish for grilling. In the first method called shioyaki, the fish is well salted before grilling, and in the second called terriyaki the fish is marinated in a sauce before or after grilling or basted with a sauce during grilling.

Shioyaki

Salted, grilled fish is the simplest of dishes. The salt helps to keep the flesh moist and, without any other adornment, the natural flavour of the fish can be appreciated to the full.

Trout Grilled with Salt (Ayu Shioyaki)

4 fresh trout
Salt
Oil

Clean and scale fish, but leave on head and tail. Skewer fish
as described and lightly salt all over (the correct amount of
salt is 2–3% of the weight of fish). Allow to stand for 30
minutes. Pre-heat grill. Cover fish tails in silver foil to
prevent burning. Brush grill rack lightly with oil and grill the
trout six minutes on each side. Do not turn more than once.
Towards the end of grilling the second side, turn grill up and
brown fish. Remove skewers and serve.

Almost any fish or fish fillet (with skin left on) can be
cooked in this way. Seabream, if you can obtain it, is
particularly good.

Basic Terriyaki

Small whole fish of the red (oily) kind (for example,
mackerel, herring, etc.) are best for this recipe. If you use
filleted fish make sure the skin is left on.

    450 g (1 lb) whole fish, cleaned, or filleted fish
    Soy sauce
    1 lemon, thinly sliced
    50 g (2 oz) ginger root, grated (optional)

Pre-heat moderate grill. Skewer fish as described on p. 105.
Brush fish with soy sauce and grill for total of five to ten
minutes on each side, depending on size of fish. Turn fish three
to four times during cooking and each time brush with soy
sauce. The fish is cooked when the centre flesh flakes if
prodded with a fork. Remove skewers and serve fish hot,
garnished with lemon slices and grated ginger.

Terriyaki Fish with Lemon Juice and Poppy Seed

450 g (1 lb) whole fish, cleaned, or filleted fish, skin left on
2 tablespoons lemon juice
2 tablespoons vegetable oil
2 tablespoons soy sauce
3 tablespoons poppy seeds

Clean and skewer whole fish as described on p. 105 or use filleted fish. Combine lemon juice, vegetable oil and soy sauce. Brush fish with this mixture and grill as for Basic Terriyaki, substituting the lemon sauce for soy sauce. Serve sprinkled with poppy seeds. Sesame seeds may also be used.

Marinated Terriyaki

450 g (1 lb) small whole fish or filleted fish, skins left on
1 lemon, cut into 4 wedges

MARINADE
100 ml (4 fl oz) sake or white wine
100 ml (4 fl oz) soy sauce
1 tablespoon sugar
1 clove garlic, crushed

Combine ingredients of marinade together and bring to the boil. Remove from heat. Marinate fish in mixture for one hour (or more in a refrigerator). Occasionally move fish around to ensure each piece is well marinated. Pre-heat moderate grill. Cook fish flesh side up for five to ten minutes, depending on size of fish. Carefully turn fish over and baste top side with marinade. Grill another three to four minutes. In the meantime bring remaining marinade to the boil. Serve fish in individual bowls and pour over a little hot marinade sauce. Garnish with a wedge of lemon.

Grilled White Fish with Glaze

450 g (1 lb) filleted white fish, cut into four pieces
Salt
1 egg yolk
½ teaspoon salt
1 teaspoon mirin or sherry

Sprinkle fillets with salt and leave for one hour. Wipe off salt and extracted moisture with dry, clean cloth. Combine egg yolk, salt and mirin. Pre-heat moderate grill. Put fillet pieces on a skewer and brush both sides with egg yolk mixture. Grill for five to ten minutes each side, depending on size of fish. Turn once only. Serve immediately fish is cooled and glaze has hardened.

Alternatively, the fish can be prepared by the Basic Terriyaki method (see p. 109), then dressed in egg yolk mixture just before serving.

Grilled Shrimps

450 g (1 lb) large raw shrimps
75 ml (3 fl oz) soy sauce
1 tablespoon sugar
3 tablespoons sherry or mirin
Black pepper to taste

Shell and devein shrimps. Divide among four skewers. Combine soy sauce, sugar and mirin and bring to the boil. Remove from heat. Pre-heat hot grill. Brush soy sauce mixture over shrimps and cook under hot grill, basting continuously with sauce, until shrimps are tender and well glazed (two to three minutes). Season with pepper and serve.

For variety, thread shrimps with alternate mouth-size pieces of bamboo shoot, lotus root or aubergine. Grill in the same way. Prawns, shelled and deveined, may also be cooked in this manner.

Grilled Prawns

    8 large prawns
    ½ teaspoon salt
    2 tablespoons soy sauce
    2 tablespoons sake or white wine
    1 teaspoon sesame seeds
    2 tablespoons lemon juice

Wash prawns well, cut off head and legs, leave tails intact. Cut through underflesh along length of shell and open prawns flat. Salt and sprinkle with soy sauce and sake. Allow to stand 15 minutes. Pre-heat moderate grill. Sprinkle prawns with sesame seeds and cook flesh side up for four to five minutes. Turn and grill shell side for two to three minutes. Serve sprinkled with lemon juice.

Alternatively, leave out sesame seeds and season cooked prawns with a pinch of powdered ginger before sprinkling on lemon juice. The fresh garnishings recommended for sashimi (see p. 107) are also excellent accompaniments to grilled prawns.

Fried Fish

Fried Mackerel

Fish dipped in egg, coated with breadcrumbs and deep fried is a general way of cooking fish, and the Japanese use a similar method except they replace breadcrumbs with dried cooked rice.

    4 mackerel fillets (or other fish), total weight about
        450 g (1 lb)
    Cornflour
    1 egg white, beaten
    Cooked rice, washed, dried and separated into individual
        grains *or* breadcrumbs
    Oil for deep frying

Clean and dry the fillets and cut each into two pieces. Dust with cornflour, brush with egg white and roll in cooked rice or breadcrumbs. Heat oil (3.75 cm, $1\frac{1}{2}$ in deep or more) to 175°C (350°F) or until you see a slight haze forming above the oil. Drop fish in and deep fry until well cooked (six to eight minutes). Drain on absorbent paper and serve with one or more of the following accompaniments. Place each of the seasonings below in a separate bowl.

Salt
Togarashi or black pepper
7-spices pepper or cayenne
Soy sauce
2 tablespoons lemon juice
2 tablespoons sesame seeds, toasted and pounded to a
    paste in suribachi or mortar
50 g (2 oz) ginger root, grated

Before eating, dip pieces of fried fish in one or a combination of seasonings.

Deep Fried Prawns

12 large prawns
Salt
Cornflour
Cooked rice, washed, dried and separated into individual
    grains *or* breadcrumbs
1 egg white, beaten
2 medium green peppers, de-seeded, cut into 1.25 cm
    ($\frac{1}{2}$ in) thick strips
Oil for deep frying

Clean prawns, remove shells, leaving tails intact, devein, and score the undersides with a sharp knife to prevent curling during cooking. Dust with cornflour, brush with egg white and roll in cooked rice or breadcrumbs. Heat oil to 175°C

(350°F) or until you see a slight haze forming above the oil.
Deep fry prawns for one or two minutes. Drain on absorbent
paper. Meanwhile, briefly (one minute) deep fry green
pepper strips without any coating. Arrange prawns and
pepper in separate bowls and serve. This dish may also be
served with the following dipping sauce:

  100 ml (4 fl oz) soup stock or dashi
  4 tablespoons soy sauce
  2 tablespoons mirin or sherry

Combine ingredients and bring to the boil. Remove from
heat and serve as above.

Deep Fried Prawns Coated with Noodles

Proceed as for Deep Fried Prawns, but replace cooked rice
with 50 g (2 oz) somen or vermicelli broken into 0.5 cm
(¼ in) pieces. The deep fried green pepper is optional.

Deep Fried Shrimps

Shrimps may be substituted for prawns in any of the deep
fried recipes. To prepare shrimps, shell, leaving tail on,
devein, and score with sharp knife across inside curve to
prevent curling during cooking.

Fried Fish in Sauce

  175 ml (6 fl oz) fish stock or dashi
  1 tablespoon mirin or sherry
  2 tablespoons soy sauce
  450 g (1 lb) filleted fish, cut into 5 cm (2 in) × 2.5 cm (1 in)
    pieces
  Cornflour
  Oil for deep frying

Combine stock or dashi, mirin or soy sauce, bring to the boil, reduce heat and simmer. Dust fish pieces in cornflour. Heat oil to 175°C (350°F) or until you see a slight haze forming above the oil. Deep fry fish for five to six minutes. Remove and drain on absorbent paper. Add fish to simmering sauce and simmer for a further 10–15 minutes. Serve fish in individual bowls with sauce poured over.

Marinated Fried Fish

175 ml (6 fl oz) fish stock or dashi
3 tablespoons vinegar
2 teaspoons sugar
1 tablespoon soy sauce
Pinch of salt and togarashi or black pepper
450 g (1 lb) filleted fish, cut into 5 cm (2 in) × 2.5 cm (1 in) pieces
Cornflour
Oil for deep frying

Combine first six ingredients and bring to the boil. Remove from heat and cool. Dust fish with cornflower. Heat oil to 175°C (350°F) or until you see a slight haze forming above the oil. Deep fry fish for one minute. Remove and drain on absorbent paper. Marinate fish in cooked sauce for two to three hours. Serve hot or cold.

Salmon Fishcakes

100 g (4 oz) tinned salmon *or* fresh salmon, poached
1 small leek, finely chopped
1 medium carrot, finely shredded
12 g (½ oz) ginger root, grated (optional)
Salt and black pepper to taste
2 eggs, beaten

Cornflour
Oil for deep frying
Soy sauce

Combine first four ingredients and mash together. Season to taste with salt and black pepper. Stir in eggs and mix well. Heat oil to 175°C (350°F) or until you see a haze forming above the oil. Form fish mixture into mouth-sized balls or patties, dust with cornflour and deep fry until golden brown. Drain on absorbent paper and serve with soy sauce. Other tinned (for example tuna, or crab) or cooked fish can be used in this recipe.

Baked Fish

Baked Fish with Vegetables

The Japanese method of baking fish is very simple and it preserves all the flavour of the fish. It was developed to make use of oven-top burners since the Japanese do not normally use ovens. Cooked on top of the stove or in the oven this is a complete and tasty dish.

4 shiitake or 4 large mushrooms
450 g (1 lb) filleted white fish or salmon
1 medium onion, sliced
2 medium green peppers, de-seeded and quartered
1 lemon, sliced
Salt and black pepper
4 teaspoons sake or white wine (optional)
Soy sauce

Soak shiitake in cold water for 20 minutes. Cut away any hard stems and criss-cross caps with shallow knife cuts. Alternatively, use fresh mushrooms with stems removed. Cut fish into four pieces and prepare four pieces of aluminium foil about 15 × 25 cm (6 in × 10 in). Lightly grease foil and, on each piece, lay in order a portion of: onion slices, fish, green pepper and shiitake or mushrooms. Season with salt, pepper and sake, top with a slice of lemon and wrap tightly in foil. Wrap each foil parcel in another piece of foil. Pre-heat frying pan over a moderate heat, place in wrapped fish, cover and cook for 10–12 minutes. Alternatively, bake foil parcels in a pre-heated oven 220°C (425°F) for 15–20 minutes. Serve in foil with soy sauce for seasoning. For variety, thinly sliced aubergine may be added to the vegetables baked with the fish.

Baked Trout with Vegetables

Follow recipe as for Baked Fish with Vegetables, but replace white fish with four fresh trout. To prepare trout for cooking, clean, score skin on one side with three knife cuts, sprinkle lightly with salt, allow to stand for 10–15 minutes. Then clean off salt with dry cloth and proceed as directed in the recipe.

Boiled, Simmered or Casseroled Fish Dishes

The Japanese use two methods of casseroling. In the first, all ingredients are combined and cooked together. In the second, each ingredient is cooked separately in the stock, removed, kept warm, and arranged at the table around the stock which is then used as a dipping sauce.

Fish Casserole I

    4 shiitake or 4 large, fresh mushrooms
    450 g (1 lb) fresh fish, filleted
    1 medium onion, thinly sliced
    1 bamboo shoot, cut into thin half-moon shapes

1 medium carrot, cut into 2.5 cm (1 in) lengths
1 clove garlic, crushed
850 ml (1½ pt) water or fish stock
25 g (1 oz) ginger root, grated
Salt and black pepper to taste
175 g (6 oz) tofu, 2.5 cm (1 in) cubes
2 small leeks or spring onions, 2.5 cm (1 in) pieces
4 tablespoons soy sauce
Juice of 1 lemon (optional)
2 tablespoons mirin or sherry (optional)

Soak shiitake in cold water for 20 minutes. Cut away hard stems. Reserve soaking water and use as part of water or stock for recipe. Alternatively, use fresh mushrooms. Cut fish into 8 equal pieces, combine in a casserole dish with shiitake, onion, bamboo shoot, carrot, garlic, water or stock, ginger root and salt and black pepper to taste. Bring to the boil, reduce heat, cover and simmer for 15 minutes. Now add tofu and leeks and simmer a further two minutes. Mix soy sauce, lemon and mirin and divide among four small bowls. Put casserole dish directly on to table, invite guests to lift out with chopsticks, pieces of cooked fish or vegetable and dip into soy sauce/lemon mixture before eating. Finally, to finish off, ladle stock into bowls for your guests to drink. For variety, replace ginger root with 100 g (4 oz) tomato purée.

Fish Casserole II

575 ml (1 pt) water or fish stock
4 tablespoons sugar
4 tablespoons soy sauce
450 g (1 lb) fresh fish, filleted, cut into 8 equal pieces
1 medium onion, thinly sliced
1 bamboo shoot, cut into half-moon shapes

1 medium carrot, cut into 2.5 cm (1 in) lengths
175 g (6 oz) tofu, cut into 2.5 cm (1 in) cubes
2 small leeks or spring onions in 2.5 cm (1 in) lengths
100 g (4 oz) greens (e.g. spinach, broccoli, Brussels
    sprouts), chopped

Combine water, soy sauce and sugar and bring to the boil.
Reduce heat and simmer. Pre-heat moderate oven. Separately
cook each of the other ingredients in the soy sauce stock.
Remove after cooking and store in warm oven. Divide
cooked ingredients among four bowls and serve cooking
liquid as dipping sauce. Alternatively, arrange fish in centre
of large serving dish, surround with cooked vegetables and
serve with dipping sauce as above. Other vegetables than
those suggested can be used in Fish Casserole I or II. For
instance, try cabbage, peas, turnip, green peppers, etc.

Herring Simmered with Sweet Soy Sauce

    4 whole fresh herring, about 900 g (2 lb)
    50 g (2 oz) sugar
    100 ml (4 fl oz) sake or white wine
    50 ml (4 fl oz) soy sauce
    25 g (1 oz) ginger root, grated
    100 g (4 oz) French beans, parboiled in a little salted water
        or 100 g (4 oz) fresh garden peas, cooked

Clean herring and remove heads. In a wide pan, bring sugar,
sake, soy sauce and ginger to the boil. Place fish in pan and
return to the boil. Reduce heat and very gently simmer for
20–25 minutes, or until nearly all the liquid has been
absorbed or evaporated. Carefully remove fish to a large
serving plate and serve garnished with French beans or
garden peas. Mackerel can also be cooked in this way.

White Fish Simmered in Miso

450 g (1 lb) filleted white fish
Cornflour
4 tablespoons vegetable oil
1 clove garlic, crushed
4 tablespoons miso
225 ml (8 fl oz) water
25 g (1 oz) ginger root, grated
100 ml (4 fl oz) soy sauce
1 tablespoon sugar
Juice of 1 lemon

Cut fish into four pieces and dust with cornflour. Heat oil in a heavy frying pan, add garlic and sauté for one minute. Now fry fish on both sides until well browned. Cream miso with a little water and add it with remaining water, soy sauce, ginger and sugar to pan. Bring to the boil, reduce heat and simmer for 15–20 minutes or until all the liquid has been absorbed or evaporated. Transfer to a large serving dish and serve hot, sprinkled with lemon juice. Serve this dish with plain fried bean sprouts (see p. 81).

Boiled Prawns

12 large prawns
4 tablespoons soy sauce
4 tablespoons water
Pinch of salt
1 tablespoon mirin or sherry (optional)

Clean prawns. Remove heads, leave tails intact. Combine soy sauce, water, salt and mirin, bring to the boil and add prawns. Gently boil prawns until they turn pink (four to six minutes). Drain, reserve liquid. Serve prawns in individual bowls with cooking liquid as dipping sauce.

Boiled Shrimps

Proceed as for Boiled Prawns but replace prawns with 225 g (8 oz) shrimps.

Sweet and Sour Prawns

    12 large prawns
    225 ml (8 fl oz) water
    3 tablespoons vinegar
    1 tablespoon sugar
    3 tablespoons soy sauce
    1 teaspoon salt
    1 tablespoon sesame seeds, toasted
    25 g (1 oz) ginger root, grated (optional)

Clean prawns. Remove heads, leave tails intact. Bring water to the boil, drop in prawns and gently boil until they turn pink (four to six minutes). Drain. Combine vinegar, sugar, soy sauce and salt, bring to the boil and remove from heat. Marinate prawns in this mixture for one to two hours. Serve garnished with sesame seeds and ginger.

Steamed Fish

Fish Steamed with Salt

Very simple and effective way of cooking fish.

    450 g (1 lb) white fish, scaled and cleaned
    1 tablespoon salt
    3 tablespoons soy sauce
    1 tablespoon vinegar
    1 tablespoon lemon juice
    175 g (6 oz) small turnip or daikon, grated
    1 small, young leek, thinly sliced

Score flesh of fish with sharp knife cuts and sprinkle with salt. Place in steamer or colander inside pan (see pp. 17–18) and steam for 20–30 minutes or until cooked. Prepare dipping sauce by combining soy sauce, vinegar and lemon juice. Serve fish with small bowls of grated turnip and leek and a central bowl of dipped sauce.

POULTRY
AND MEAT

Originally because of tradition, and now as a result of geography and economics, beef has never been very common in Japan. Chicken and pigs take up less land, and do not need large areas of pasture. The Japanese housewife never buys a joint of meat in the way we may do in the West. She probably wouldn't have an oven to cook it in, and anyway pork and beef are ususally eaten sparingly, combined with vegetables and rice.

Pork is normally bought lean, in small amounts or as pork cutlets (chops). Beef is cut wafer-thin by the butcher, and cut into mouth-sized amounts before serving. Chicken can be bought ready boned and consequently many Japanese recipes requiring chicken specify lean flesh. If you cannot find a poulterer who will bone your chicken for you (very likely these days), either cut the chicken into pieces as described below and leave the bones in, or buy chicken breasts and bone as follows. Hold the breast skin side down, bend it backwards in half until it is flat on the work surface. Pull out the central bone that pops up and cut the breast into two pieces (ignore this if the chicken breasts are already separated). Press the blade of a sharp pointed knife under the base of the ribs of breast, and gently cut away from the flesh as you pull bone upwards. Continue along rib bones until you have detached entire rib cage from flesh.

To cut chicken into pieces, separate it with a meat cleaver into: legs, thighs, wings, breast and back. Cut each joint into two pieces except the back: cut this into four pieces. You should end up with twenty pieces of chicken. Remember, all meat and poultry is easier to cut, etc., when slightly frozen.

The chapter is arranged under chicken, pork and beef headings, and these are sub-divided into cooking methods used, e.g. grilling, frying, boiling, etc. Grilling is a popular Japanese way of cooking meat. Traditionally, this would have been done over a charcoal brazier, and many of the poultry and meat recipes are suitable for barbecues.

Chicken

Grilled Chicken (Yaki Tori)

Small pieces of chicken flesh, liver or other parts of the giblets are marinated in a barbecue-type sauce, threaded on to small bamboo or metal skewers and grilled. Yaki tori is a popular Japanese snack which, along with other food cooked on skewers, they call 'kebabs'.

Serve yaki tori as a starter to a meal or, for a more substantial dish, grill vegetables along with the chicken and serve over rice. Cook under a gas or electric grill or in barbecue fashion over a charcoal brazier.

    2 medium-size chicken breasts, boned
    3 tablespoons soy sauce
    2 tablespoons sugar
    1 teaspoon powdered ginger
    1 clove garlic, crushed
    1 teaspoon oil

Cut the chicken into mouth-size pieces. Combine the other ingredients except the oil, and bring to the boil. Remove from the heat and marinate chicken in the mixture for 30 minutes or more. Lightly oil the skewers and thread on chicken pieces. Grill for six to eight minutes. Turn once or twice and brush with marinade from time to time. Serve well browned, sprinkled with any remaining marinade.

Chicken on Skewers with Vegetables

In this recipe, apart from the flesh, the liver and skin of the chicken are also used. The Japanese, if they eat meat, are not squeamish about what parts of the animal they eat, and tend to make good use of all edible parts.

450 g (1 lb) chicken breast, boned *or* other lean chicken flesh
100 g (4 oz) chicken livers
2 cloves garlic, crushed
575 ml (1 pt) water
2 medium green peppers, de-seeded and quartered
1 medium onion, cut into mouth-size pieces
2 leeks, cut into 2.5 cm (1 in) lengths
1 teaspoon oil
100 ml (4 fl oz) soy sauce
100 ml (4 fl oz) mirin or sherry
1½ tablespoons sugar
Togarashi or black pepper to taste

Remove skin from chicken breasts, and cut flesh into mouth-size pieces. Cut skin into 2.5 cm (1 in) squares. Add one clove garlic to water and bring to the boil. Quarter chicken livers and drop into boiling water. Remove after 30 seconds with slotted spoon and put to one side. Boil chicken skin in the same water for one minute. Drain. Combine remaining garlic, soy sauce, mirin and sugar and bring to the boil. Reduce heat and simmer. Meanwhile, divide chicken flesh, liver, skin and vegetable pieces into four portions. Oil four skewers and thread on each a piece of chicken, vegetable, skin, vegetable, liver, etc. Repeat until all the meat and vegetables have been used up. Remove sauce from heat and in it marinade skewered ingredients for 30 minutes or more. Pre-heat hot grill. Grill skewered food for six to eight minutes. Turn once or twice and brush from time to time with marinade. Serve well browned, seasoned to taste with togarashi or black pepper, with bowls of boiled rice.

An alternative way of serving this dish is to skewer all the ingredients separately and to arrange the skewers of cooked food around a central bed of rice. Allow the guests to help themselves to whatever combination of chicken or vegetable pieces they wish.

Chicken Terriyaki

Pieces of chicken are marinated in a sauce, fried and then simmered in more marinade until cooked. A simple, but very effective cooking method.

    900 g (2 lb) chicken, cut into pieces (retaining skin)
    100 ml (4 fl oz) soy sauce
    50 ml (2 fl oz) mirin and 50 ml (2 fl oz) sake *or* 100 ml
       (4 fl oz) dry sherry
    25 g (1 oz) ginger root, grated
    1 clove garlic, crushed
    2 tablespoons vegetable oil
    1 lemon, quartered

Pierce the skin on each piece of chicken in two or three places. Combine remaining ingredients, except oil and lemon, and bring to the boil. Remove from the heat and marinate chicken pieces in mixture for 30 minutes or more. Remove chicken and shake off excess liquid. Reserve marinade. Heat oil in heavy frying pan over a medium heat. Add chicken pieces, skin side down. Fry until browned, turn over, reduce heat, cover and simmer for ten minutes.

Remove chicken from pan and discard any liquid that has collected. Return chicken to pan, pour over remaining marinade and simmer uncovered until all liquid has been absorbed or evaporated. Serve with wedges of lemon.

For variety serve the chicken with lightly sautéed green peppers, or a raw vegetable salad, such as cucumber, radish and celery.

Sauté Chicken (Niwa Tori)

6 tablespoons soy sauce
2 tablespoons sugar
4 tablespoons water
½ teaspoon 7-spices pepper or cayenne
1 clove garlic, crushed
900 g (2 lb) chicken cut into pieces
2 tablespoons vegetable oil
2 spring onions, finely chopped *or* 2 tablespoons chives, chopped

Combine first six ingredients and bring to the boil. Remove from heat and marinate chicken in mixture for 30 minutes or more. Remove chicken and reserve marinade. Drain chicken on absorbent paper. Heat oil in a heavy frying pan and fry chicken for six to eight minutes, turning several times during cooking. Finally, add spring onions or chives, cook for a further minute and serve over hot rice and sprinkle with remaining marinade.

Deep Fried Chicken

Ingredients as for Sauté Chicken (see above) plus cornflour. Oil for deep frying.

Marinate chicken as in recipe above. Remove from marinade, shake off excess liquid but do not wipe. Dust with cornflour and set aside. Heat oil to 175°C (350°F) or until you see a light haze forming above the oil. Deep fry chicken, a few pieces at a time until golden brown. Drain on absorbent paper. Serve with the spring onion or chives, either fresh or lightly sautéed.

Spiced Sauté Chicken with Vegetables

    2 tablespoons vegetable oil
    25 g (1 oz) ginger root, grated
    2 chilli peppers de-seeded, shredded *or* ½ teaspoon hot
      pepper sauce
    900 g (2 lb) chicken cut into pieces
    1 medium onion, diced
    1 medium carrot, thinly sliced
    100 g (4 oz) mushrooms, sliced
    1 bamboo shoot, diced
    4 tablespoons soy sauce
    100 ml (4 fl oz) chicken stock or water
    2 tablespoons sugar
    100 g (4 oz) French beans cut into 5 cm (2 in) lengths *or*
      100 g (4 oz) cooked peas

Heat oil in a heavy frying pan, add ginger and chilli peppers (but not hot pepper sauce if you are using it), and sauté for one minute. Add chicken pieces and cook for three to four minutes, turning once. Stir in, in order: onions, carrots, mushrooms and bamboo shoots, and sauté each for one minute after adding to pan. Pour in stock, soy sauce and sugar (plus hot pepper sauce if used). Reduce heat, cover and simmer for 15 to 20 minutes. Add French beans or peas and simmer a further two minutes. Serve.

Fried Chicken with Sesame Seeds

  4 chicken breasts, boned
  2 tablespoons sake or white wine
  1 tablespoon salt
  2 tablespoons vegetable oil
  2 tablespoons sesame seeds
  1 lettuce, chilled

Score skin of chicken breasts with a sharp knife and sprinkle with salt and sake. Leave to stand for 30 minutes. Heat oil in a heavy frying pan and fry chicken on both sides until well cooked and browned. Remove chicken and lightly fry sesame seeds in residual oil. Serve chicken sprinkled with sesame seeds in a bed of chilled lettuce leaves.

Twice Fried Chicken

  4 tablespoons soy sauce
  1 tablespoon mirin or sherry
  Juice 1 lemon
  1 teaspoon salt
  450 g (1 lb) chicken breast, boned, cut into 0.5 cm (¼ in)
      thick slices
  2 tablespoons vegetable oil
  4 sticks celery, chilled

Combine first four ingredients and pour over chicken slices. Marinade for one hour or more. Drain and reserve liquid. Heat oil in a heavy frying pan and lightly fry chicken on both sides. Return to marinade and leave for five minutes. Drain again and fry in same pan until nicely browned both sides. Be careful to drain thoroughly each time, since soy sauce burns easily. Serve with hot rice and sticks of chilled celery.

Chicken Croquettes (Tori Kuroke)

> 225 g (8 oz) minced chicken
> 225 g (8 oz) cooked potato, mashed
> ½ medium onion, diced
> Pinch of salt
> 1 egg, beaten
> 1 tablespoon soy sauce
> Breadcrumbs
> Oil for deep frying
> 1 sheet nori, toasted *or* 2 tablespoons sesame seeds, toasted

Combine first six ingredients and mix thoroughly. Form into bite-size balls and roll in breadcrumbs. Heat oil to 175°C (350°F) or until you see a light haze forming above the oil. Deep fry croquettes, a few at a time, until golden brown. Drain on absorbent paper and serve sprinkled with crumbled nori or sesame seeds.

Aubergines with Chicken Sauce

> 4 small aubergines
> 2 tablespoons vegetable oil
> 225 g (8 oz) minced chicken
> 2 tablespoons sugar
> 100 ml (4 fl oz) chicken stock or water
> 2 tablespoons miso
> 2 tablespoons sake or white wine (optional)

Cut aubergines almost in half but leave stem end intact. Score shiny sides with sharp knife cuts. Brush all over with some of the oil. Pre-heat moderate grill. Open aubergines to show as much inside surface as possible and grill until just soft. Turn once during cooking. Heat a heavy pan and brush with remaining oil, add chicken and sauté over moderate heat for one minute. Cream the miso with a little of the stock and add this and all the remaining ingredients to the pan. Stir well and simmer for eight to ten minutes. Arrange egg plants, half open, in individual bowls. Pour over chicken sauce and serve.

Boiled Chicken with Vegetables

4 dried shiitake *or* 100 g (4 oz) mushrooms
450 g (1 lb) chicken cut into pieces
2 tablespoons sugar
2 tablespoons soy sauce
4 tablespoons mirin or sherry
100 ml (4 fl oz) chicken stock or water
1 medium carrot, cut into matchsticks
100 g (4 oz) bamboo shoots, cut into half moons
100 g (4 oz) water chestnuts

Soak shiitake in cold water for 20 minutes. Drain, cut away hard stems and thinly slice. Otherwise use sliced mushrooms. Combine sugar, soy sauce, mirin and stock and bring to the boil. Add chicken, return to the boil, reduce heat, cover and simmer for 30-40 minutes or until chicken is tender. Remove chicken pieces from pan and add to it the shiitake, carrot, bamboo shoots and water chestnuts. Return to the boil, reduce heat, cover and simmer until carrots are tender. Return chicken to the pan and gently heat uncovered until nearly all the liquid has evaporated. Serve.

Chicken and Shrimp with Lemon Dipping Sauce

175 ml (6 fl oz) chicken stock or water
2 tablespoons soy sauce
2 tablespoons sugar
4 large shrimps, shelled
225 g (8 oz) lean chicken meat, diced

225 g (8 oz) bamboo shoots, cut into thin half moons
2 medium green peppers, de-seeded and quartered
2 small leeks, cut into 2.5 cm (1 in) lengths
175 g (6 oz) tofu, 2.5 cm (1 in) cubes (optional)
3 tablespoons lemon juice

Pre-heat moderate oven. Combine stock, soy sauce and sugar, bring to the boil and add shrimps. Poach for two to three minutes. Remove shrimps and add chicken pieces to same liquid, return to the boil, reduce heat and cook chicken until tender. Repeat with each of the vegetables and tofu and store each cooked item in oven to keep warm. Now reduce cooking liquid, over moderate heat, to half its volume, add lemon juice, bring to the boil and remove from heat. Arrange chicken, shrimps, vegetables and tofu in colourful pattern on a large plate and serve with lemon sauce for dipping.

Prawns may be used in place of shrimps.

Deep Fried Chicken in Broth

Oil for deep frying
450 g (1 lb) chicken, cut into pieces
Cornflour
850 ml (1½ pt) chicken stock
2 tablespoons soy sauce
2 tablespoons sugar
25 g (1 oz) ginger root, grated
225 g (8 oz) Chinese cabbage, shredded
2 medium green peppers, de-seeded, cut into 2.5 cm (1 in) wide strips
100 g (4 oz) mushrooms, whole
½ bunch watercress or parsley, chopped

Heat oil to 175°C (350°F) or until you see a slight haze forming above the oil. Dust chicken with cornflour and deep fry golden brown. Remove from oil and drain on absorbent paper. Combine chicken with remaining ingredients except watercress or parsley and bring to the boil. Reduce heat and simmer until vegetables are cooked. Serve in individual bowls garnished with watercress or parsley.

Baked Chicken and Mushrooms

Like the Baked Fish dish (see pp. 116–17) this way of baking chicken was devised to be used on top of the stove. It really preserves the flavour of the cooked foods. In a Western kitchen, oven baking is more convenient and just as good as the original way of cooking.

4 chicken legs or breasts
1 teaspoon salt
4 shiitake *or* 4 large fresh mushrooms
1 lemon cut into 4 slices
1 tablespoon vegetable oil
1 young leek or 2 spring onions, thinly sliced
100 ml (4 fl oz) soy sauce
100 ml (4 fl oz) lemon juice

Soak shiitake for 20 minutes in cold water. Cut away hard stems and criss-cross caps with shallow knife cuts. Otherwise use fresh mushrooms with stems removed. Sprinkle salt on chicken and mushrooms. Pre-heat oven to 190°C (370°F). Cut out 4 pieces of aluminium foil large enough to wrap each chicken piece. Brush one side of each piece of foil with oil, and arrange on top a piece of chicken topped with one mushroom and one lemon slice. Wrap securely and bake in oven for 30 minutes. Meanwhile, prepare dipping sauce. Combine soy sauce and lemon juice and divide among four small bowls. Add a portion of chopped leek to each. Serve each foil wrapped chicken parcel with a small dish of dipping sauce.

Grilled Pork (Buta Terriyaki)

Terriyaki dishes always involve some marinating process in a sauce that nearly always includes, among other things, soy sauce, sugar and garlic. Here we give recipes for two terriyaki sauces. Sauce I is sweeter than Sauce II. Both sauces can be made more spicy by the addition of a little chopped chilli pepper or a dash of hot pepper sauce.

    450 g (1 lb) lean pork, cut into 2.5 cm (1 in) cubes
    2 tablespoons sesame seeds, toasted (optional)

SAUCE I
    100 ml (4 fl oz) soy sauce
    2 tablespoons mirin or sweet sherry
    1 clove garlic, crushed
    1 teaspoon sugar

SAUCE II
    175 ml (6 fl oz) soy sauce
    25 g (1 oz) ginger root, grated *or* 1 teaspoon powdered
      ginger
    1 clove garlic, crushed
    Juice of 1 lemon
    1 tablespoon sugar

Combine ingredients of Sauce I or II and marinate pork in mixture for one or two hours. Pre-heat medium grill. Remove pork from marinade and grill until nicely brown on all sides. Baste with marinade during grilling. Serve garnished with sesame seeds over hot boiled rice. Accompany with grilled vegetables, for example green peppers, onions, mushrooms, etc.

Crispy Fried Pork

Ingredients as for Grilled Pork plus cornflour, oil for deep frying. Marinate pork as for Grilled Pork. Remove pork from marinade but do not wipe. Coat each piece with cornflour. Heat oil to 175°C (350°F) or until you see a slight haze forming above the oil. Deep fry the pork a few pieces at a time until golden brown. Drain on absorbent paper and serve as for Grilled Pork.

Pork Kebabs

Strangely, traditional Japanese pork kebabs are deep fried and not grilled. Cubes of lean pork are skewered with a selection of vegetables, dipped in flour, egg white, bread-crumbs and deep fried. The vegetables given in the recipe are suggestions only, and you may add or substitute others.

450 g (1 lb) lean pork, cut into 1.25 cm ($\frac{1}{2}$ in) cubes
1 small aubergine, cut into 2.5 cm (1 in) cubes
2 medium green peppers cut into 2.5 cm (1 in) squares
100 g (4 oz) small mushrooms, left whole
2 leeks, cut into 2.5 cm (1 in) lengths
8 baby onions
Salt and black pepper to taste
Flour
2 eggs, beaten
Breadcrumbs
Oil for frying
Soy sauce

Oil four or more skewers and string on to each pieces of pork and vegetables in an attractive, colourful order. Season with salt and black pepper. Dust each with flour, brush with egg and roll in breadcrumbs. Set aside. Heat oil to 175°C (350°F) or until you see a light haze forming above the oil. Deep fry kebabs a few at a time for four to five minutes or until golden brown. Serve with soy sauce.

Fried Pork Cutlets

If she wants to cook pork, apart from buying a few slices of lean pork, the Japanese housewife is most likely to purchase pork cutlets. The cutlet is cooked, then boned and the lean meat cut into mouth-size pieces. Frying is the simplest and most common cooking method.

> 450 g (1 lb) pork cutlets
> 2 eggs, beaten
> Breadcrumbs
> Oil for frying
> Soy sauce

Brush cutlets with beaten egg, and roll in breadcrumbs. Set aside. Heat 0.5 cm (¼ in) oil in a heavy frying pan and fry cutlets for five to six minutes, or until golden brown, turning once during cooking. Remove, drain on absorbent paper, cut meat away from bones and into mouth-size pieces. Serve over hot rice with soy sauce.

Pork Cutlet Donburi (Katsudon)

This recipe is similar to the one above, but a little more elaborate and substantial. It is a popular lunchtime meal.

> 225 ml (8 fl oz) soup stock or water
> 100 ml (4 fl oz) soy sauce
> 3 tablespoons sugar
> 2 tablespoons mirin or sherry (optional)
> 1 medium onion, diced
> 450 g (1 lb) Fried Pork Cutlets (see recipe above)
> 4 eggs, beaten

225 g (8 oz) bean sprouts
450 g (1 lb) cooked rice

Pre-heat moderate oven. Combine first four ingredients and bring to the boil. Add onion, reduce heat and simmer. Prepare Fried Pork Cutlets (see recipe above), and set aside in oven to keep warm. Drain most of the oil from the pan in which the cutlets were cooked, and add bean sprouts, cooking until just soft. Pour in beaten eggs and lightly scramble. Pour boiling water over cooked rice, drain and divide rice among four bowls. Top each with a portion of bean sprouts and egg, crown with pork cutlets and pour over each a portion of the simmering sauce and onion. Do not use all the sauce if it means causing liquid to form in the bottom of the bowls. Serve.

Pork Cutlets with Sesame Seeds

3 tablespoons sesame seeds, toasted
4 tablespoons sake or white wine
4 tablespoons soy sauce
1 clove garlic, crushed
1 tablespoon sugar
2 tablespoons vegetable oil
450 g (1 lb) pork cutlets
1 tablespoon wasabi or English mustard paste

Crush sesame seeds in a suribachi or mortar, add garlic, sake, soy sauce and sugar. Mix well. Heat oil in a heavy frying pan, add pork cutlets and brown on both sides. Reduce heat and evenly cover the top of each cutlet with sesame seed mixture. Cover pan and cook for three to four minutes. Serve with small bowl of wasabi or mustard.

Hot Fried Pork (Buta Yaki)

For this dish you do not need lean meat and any soft fat is complemented by the recommended fresh chilled side salad.

    2 tablespoons soy sauce
    2 tablespoons sake or white wine
    2 tablespoons sesame seeds, pounded to a paste in
      suribachi or mortar
    $1/2$–1 chilli pepper, shredded
    450 g (1 lb) pork, sliced 0.5 cm ($1/4$ in) thick

Combine the first four ingredients and marinate the pork in the mixture for one hour. Remove pork from marinade, cut into 2.5 cm (1 in) square pieces. Heat oil in heavy frying pan and fry pork squares until brown on both sides. Divide pork among four bowls, sprinkle with remaining marinade. Toss salad in dressing and serve with bowls of pork.

SALAD
    50 g (2 oz) cooked somen or vermicelli
    100 g (4 oz) cucumber, sliced
    2 tomatoes, thinly sliced

DRESSING
    2 tablespoons vinegar
    1 teaspoon black pepper
    1 tablespoon sugar

Prepare the salad by mixing somen, cucumber and tomatoes. Store in refrigerator. Make dressing by mixing vinegar, black pepper and sugar. Set aside until about to be eaten, then toss.

Pork Meat Balls

    4 shiitake or 100 g (4 oz) mushrooms
    450 g (1 lb) minced pork

½ medium onion diced
1 egg, beaten
4 tablespoons soy sauce
1 teaspoon sugar
½ teaspoon salt
1 tablespoon flour
1 tablespoon wasabi or English mustard paste
Oil for deep frying

Soak the shiitake for 20 minutes. Cut away hard stem and
chop finely. Otherwise use finely chopped mushrooms.
Combine pork, shiitake, onion, egg, one tablespoon soy
sauce, sugar, salt and flour and mix well. Form into bite-size
balls. Heat oil to 175°C (350°F) or until you see a slight haze
forming above the oil. Deep fry meatballs a few at a time
until golden brown. Drain on absorbent paper. Mix wasabi
with three tablespoons soy sauce and serve as a dipping
sauce for meatballs.

Pork and Apple Meatballs

Proceed as for Pork Meatballs but replace onion with one
medium apple, grated.

Fried Pork Stew

450 g (1 lb) lean pork, cut into 2.5 cm (1 in) cubes
2 tablespoons vegetable oil
Cornflour
1 medium onion, sliced
2 medium carrots, 1.25 cm (½ in) thick slices
225 g (8 oz) Chinese cabbage or drumhead cabbage,
    shredded
2 sticks celery, chopped
450 ml (1 pt) chicken stock

2 tablespoons soy sauce
2 teaspoons sugar
1 teaspoon salt
1 tablespoon sake or white wine (optional)

Heat oil in a heavy frying pan. Dust pork with cornflour and fry, stirring frequently, for three to four minutes. Transfer pork to another pan and fry onions until lightly browned in the same frying pan. Add onions and remaining ingredients to pork, bring to the boil, reduce heat, cover and simmer until pork and vegetables are cooked (about fifteen to twenty minutes). Serve with separate bowls of boiled rice. Other vegetables may be added or substituted in the stew.

Pork with Deep Fried Tofu

The fried tofu (aburage) absorbs the flavour of the vegetables and meat and unites them.

2 tablespoons vegetable oil
225 g (8 oz) pork, cut into 2.5 cm (1 in) cubes
25 g (1 oz) ginger root, grated
1 medium onion, sliced
100 g (4 oz) Chinese or drumhead cabbage, shredded
350 g (12 oz) deep fried tofu (see p. 100)
4 tablespoons soy sauce
100 ml (4 oz) soup stock or water
Salt to taste

Heat oil in a heavy pan, add the pork and sauté for two to three minutes. Add the ginger, onion and cabbage and sauté a further two or three minutes. Stir in the remaining ingredients, bring to the boil, cover and simmer until pork is cooked (about 15 to 20 minutes). Serve. Other greens may be substituted for the cabbage, for example broccoli, Brussels sprouts, etc.

Beef

Grilled Beef (Yaki Niku)

    100 ml (4 fl oz) soy sauce
    1 tablespoon sugar
    1 clove garlic, crushed
    25 g (1 oz) ginger root, grated
    2 tablespoons mirin or sherry (optional)
    450 g (1 lb) lean beef, thinly sliced

Combine first five ingredients, mix well and marinate beef in mixture for one hour or more. Pre-heat medium grill. Remove beef from marinade and grill for two to four minutes (depending on how well done you wish it) on each side. Baste with marinade once or twice during cooking. Cut into 2.5 cm (1 in) strips and serve with rice and salad. Store residual marinade in sealed container in refrigerator. It keeps for up to a month.

Glazed Grilled Beef

Ingredients as for Grilled Beef (above) plus two teaspoons cornflour.

Marinate meat as above, and remove from marinade, but before grilling prepare glaze as follows. Cream cornflour with a little of the marinade. Bring remainder to the boil and stir in creamed cornflour, continue heating until marinade has thickened and cleared. Remove from heat. Grill meat as described above, but do not baste with marinade. Cut beef into 2.5 cm (1 in) strips, arrange in a bowl or over hot boiled rice and pour over thickened marinade or glaze.

Beef Kebabs

Ingredients as for Grilled Beef (p. 141)

Marinate beef as for Grilled Beef. Remove beef from marinade and cut into 2.5–5 cm (1–2 in) squares. Thread on to skewers. Pre-heat medium grill and grill kebabs for two to three minutes each side. Baste once or twice with marinade.

For variety, grill alongside skewered beef squares, skewers of onion and green pepper or aubergines cut into suitable shapes.

Deep Fried Beef Kebabs

Ingredients as for Grilled Beef (p. 141) plus:

> 1 egg, beaten
> Breadcrumbs
> Oil for deep frying

Marinate beef as for Grilled Beef. Remove beef from marinade and cut into 2.5–5 cm (1–2 in) squares. Thread on to skewers, brush with egg and roll in breadcrumbs. Heat oil to 175°C (350°F) or until you see a light haze forming above the oil. Deep fry skewered beef until golden brown. This method may also be used for beef skewered with squares of onion and/or green pepper and/or aubergine.

Fried Beef with Fresh Vegetables

> 2 green peppers, de-seeded, thinly sliced
> 1 medium onion, thinly sliced
> ½ medium cucumber, sliced
> 1 chilli pepper, shredded (optional)
> 1 tablespoon sesame seeds, toasted
> ½ teaspoon salt
> 1 clove garlic, crushed

1 young leek, finely chopped
2 tablespoons vegetable oil
450 g (1 lb) lean beef, cut into 0.5 cm (¼ in) thick strips

Arrange green peppers, onion and cucumbers in an attractive pattern in serving bowl and chill. Pound sesame seeds in a suribachi or mortar, add the chilli pepper, salt, garlic and leek and mix well. Brush slices of beef with half this mixture. Heat oil in a heavy frying pan, add coated beef and fry until meat is tender. Serve with a fresh salad and a bowl of the remaining sesame seed mixture and boiled rice.

Deep Fried Beef with Spiced Daikon

A most unusual way of serving beef. Traditionally daikon is used. If you cannot obtain any, substitute turnips.

2 small daikon, peeled
2 chilli peppers, de-seeded, cut in half
450 g (1 lb) lean beef, cut into 5 cm × 2.5 cm (2 in × 1 in) strips
2 tablespoons sake or white wine
2 tablespoons soy sauce
Cornflour
Oil for deep frying
225 g (8 oz) French beans, parboiled in a little salted water

Make two small holes the diameter of a pencil in each end of the daikon. Push half a chilli pepper into each and leave for two to three hours. Combine sake and soy sauce and marinate beef in this mixture for one hour. Remove beef from marinade, shake off excess liquid and roll in cornflour. Set aside for a few minutes. Finely grate daikon and chill. Heat oil to 175°C (350°F) or until you see a slight haze forming above the oil. Deep fry beef until golden brown (one to two minutes). Drain on absorbent paper. Distribute beef

among four bowls, add grated daikon and garnish with
parboiled French beans.

Fried Beef with Sesame Seeds and Vegetables

225 g (8 oz) beef cut into 0.5 cm ($\frac{1}{4}$ in) thick slices
2 tablespoons sake or white wine
$\frac{1}{2}$ teaspoon salt
2–3 tablespoons vegetable oil
1 tablespoon sesame seeds
2 green peppers, de-seeded, sliced
100 g (4 oz) bean sprouts
2 stalks celery, chopped
1 small lettuce

Score surface of beef with light knife cuts. Sprinkle with salt
and sake and set aside for 15–20 minutes. Heat two
tablespoons oil in a heavy frying pan, add beef, fry until
tender and brown both sides. Remove beef from pan, add
sesame seeds and fry until light brown, stir in peppers, cook
for one minute, add bean sprouts plus remaining oil if
necessary, and cook until just wilted. Return meat to pan and
heat through. Divide contents of pan among four bowls and
serve with fresh celery and lettuce salad.

Vegetables Rolled in Beef

225 g (8 oz) lean beef, cut into 4 thin slices approximately
   5 cm × 15 cm (2 in × 6 in)
Pinch ginger powder
4 tablespoons soy sauce
1 leek, finely sliced
1 medium carrot, cut into 2.5 cm (1 in) matchsticks
1 medium green pepper, 5 cm (2 in) long by 1.25 cm ($\frac{1}{2}$ in)
   wide strips

50 g (2 oz) mushrooms, sliced
2 tablespoons vegetable oil
2 tablespoons mirin or sherry (optional)
1 small lettuce

Marinate beef in 2 tablespoons soy sauce and a pinch of ginger for 15 minutes. Lay out strips. Divide vegetables into 4 portions and arrange a layer of mixed vegetables at the end of each strip of beef. Roll up beef and vegetables and secure with a toothpick. Heat oil in a heavy frying pan and fry beef rolls well on all sides. Move toothpick back and forth if necessary. Add remaining soy sauce and mirin and fry another two minutes. Remove toothpicks and serve on a bed of lettuce.

Gyoza

Any excuse for a party was the slogan of my neighbours in Japan, and one of the dishes they always made for these enjoyable events was gyoza, spoonfuls of minced meat and vegetables wrapped in small rounds of dough, fried, and served with soy sauce.

350 g (12 oz) plain flour
Pinch of salt
4–6 tablespoons oil
175–225 ml (6–8 fl oz) water
2 cloves garlic, crushed
1 medium onion, finely diced
½ medium carrot, grated
225 g (8 oz) minced beef
Dash of hot pepper sauce (optional)
1 egg, beaten
Soy sauce to taste

Combine the flour, salt and two tablespoons oil and thoroughly mix. Add water, slowly stirring continuously until you have a firm dough. Knead well, and then roll out flat on a floured board. Cut out rounds of dough about 7.5 cm (3 in) in diameter (about 16–20). Set aside. Heat remaining oil in a heavy frying pan, add the garlic and sauté for one minute. Add onions, carrot and minced beef and fry until onions and beef are nicely browned. Remove the mixture from the pan and spoon one to two tablespoons on to each of the dough rounds. Paint the edge of each round with egg, fold one side over to meet the other. Crimp the edges together. Take each half moon shape and flatten the side without a seam to form little packages that will stand upright. Fry the gyoza in the pan in which the meat and vegetables were cooked. Add more oil if needed. Brown both sides of the gyoza and serve hot with soy sauce.

Alternatively, the gyoza can be deep fried or boiled. For deep frying see pp. 165–6. To boil, bring a large pan of water to the boil, drop the gyoza in and gently boil until they start to float to the surface. Drain and serve.

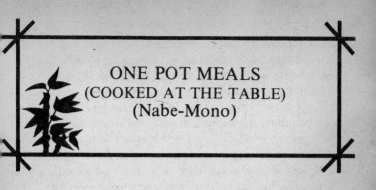

ONE POT MEALS
(COOKED AT THE TABLE)
(Nabe-Mono)

In Japanese, nabe means a pot or casserole, and nabe-mono are pot things. The name is given to complete meals prepared in a single pan or casserole, a style of cooking which lends itself admirably to the lovely Japanese tradition of cooking at the table.

In this method of cooking, the diners are involved in the preparation of the meal, and the host and hostess can spend all of their time with their guests. Cooking at the table also ensures that the food is eaten piping hot, and that it is cooked to just the degree chosen by each guest. Another attraction in Japan, where very few houses have central heating, is that the hibachi or table cooker gives off a warm glow, and what could be more pleasurable on a cold night than sitting around a charcoal burner eating hot food.

All the ingredients for a nabe-mono meal are prepared beforehand, and attractively arranged on one or two large serving dishes before laying on the table. The guests sit around the table (a low table with cushions for sitting on is the best arrangement), and the food is cooked in a frying pan or casserole over a hot plate (electric, gas, paraffin or charcoal). Frying and boiling are the two principal cooking methods used for nabe-mono. The famous table meal sukiyaki (pronounced ski-yaki) is fried and mizutaki, not well known in the West, but very popular in Japan, is boiled.

One other cooking method occasionally used is given the strange name of Mongolian or Ghengis Khan grilling. The name refers to a system of charcoal grilling at the table.

Near where I lived in Japan was a Mongolian steak house, and as I passed I always expected to see hordes of Mongolian warriors bursting through the doors. Fortunately, most of the customers didn't live up to expectations. Mongolian grilling is especially suitable for an out-of-doors barbecue.

The ingredients for a nabe-mono meal are accompanied by condiments, sauces, boiled rice and maybe a salad. Thus for a meal for four, you will ideally need the following equipment:

One low table plus four cushions
One hot plate (electric, gas, paraffin or charcoal)
One deep frying pan or large heat-proof casserole or heavy pan (an electric frying pan is ideal)
Two large serving dishes
Jugs for the cooking stock or for frying oil, and for cooking sauces
Four bowls for the main meal
Four bowls for the rice
Small dishes for sauces and salads
Four pairs of chopsticks and one pair of long cooking chopsticks
A ladle, perforated spoon and fish slice
Last, but not least, a teapot and small cups for preparing and drinking liberal amounts of tea during and after the meal:

Any special instructions applicable to a specific recipe will be given with the recipe but there are a few general tips that apply to all the nabe-mono meals. If the ingredients include fish and/or meat, they are usually cooked first to add flavour to the stock. Apart from this, start with the ingredients that need longest cooking. If, however, particular vegetables need an extra long cooking time, parboil them first. Always drain washed vegetables well, and store in a refrigerator, after preparation, until required. They should look crisp and fresh when laid on the table. Where a recipe requires very thinly sliced pieces of beef or fish this can be done more easily if the meat or fish is partially frozen before slicing it. The smell of cooking fish can be reduced by adding fresh or dried ginger root to the pan.

For each recipe, directions are given for the amounts and types of ingredients to be used, but in nabe-mono meals these things are not fixed, and you can add or substitute other ingredients. Many of the recipes require a soup stock but water plus a vegetable or meat bouillon cube may be used if you wish. As a final note, remember that all the following recipes can be cooked as equally well on a stove in a kitchen as at the table. The charm and communal warmth of cooking at the table will be lost, but the food will still taste good.

Sukiyaki

This is probably the only really well-known Japanese dish in the West. Ironically it is rarely prepared by the Japanese except for foreign guests. Never mind, it is delicious and one of my favourite meals. The name is supposed to derive from the practice by farmers of frying (yaki) their food on a metal plough (suki). There is another story, however, that Mongolian soldiers (the Japanese are said to be descendants of Mongolian stock) cooked wild game on the end of a spade (suki) over a charcoal fire.

Side dishes that usually accompany sukiyaki are miso soup (see p. 34), boiled rice (see p. 38), pickles (see p. 70), sake and green tea (pp. 180–2).

Beef Sukiyaki

One of the characteristics of beef sukiyaki is that it contains beef cut into wafer-thin slices which are then fried and dipped into raw egg before being eaten.

100 ml (4 fl oz) soy sauce
225 ml (8 fl oz) water or soup stock
3 tablespoons sugar
2 tablespoons mirin or sweet sherry
450 g (1 lb) lean beef, very thinly sliced
1 large onion, halved and sliced
2 leeks or 6 spring onions, chopped into 3.75 cm (1½ in) lengths
225 g (8 oz) mushrooms, sliced
225 g (8 oz) spinach, coarsely chopped
225 g (8 oz) Chinese or white cabbage, chopped into 1.25 cm (1 in) wide strips
175 g (6 oz) tofu, cut into 2.5 cm (1 in) squares (optional)
4 tablespoons vegetable oil
4 eggs

Combine the first four ingredients, mix well, transfer the sauce to a jug and place on the table. Arrange the remaining ingredients, except the oil, on large serving dishes and place on the table adjacent to the hot plate. Seat the guests around the table. Heat a large frying pan over the hot plate and add the oil. Wait until it's really hot, add half the beef and fry until just brown on both sides. Push beef to one side of pan, drop in half the onions and leeks and fry lightly. Add half of each of the mushrooms and cabbage. Keep each of the ingredients separate. Now pour over half the sauce and cook for three to four minutes. Add some of the tofu and spinach and cook a further two or three minutes. Meanwhile, invite each guest to break an egg into a small bowl and to whisk it lightly with chopsticks. The guests may now begin to help themselves, with their chopsticks, to the cooked food, which is dipped into the egg before being eaten. As the pan empties, replenish with uncooked ingredients and repeat the above procedure until all the food is cooked.

Beef and Aubergine Sukiyaki

This is a more straightforward recipe than the one given above. The ingredients are fried only, and no cooked liquid is used. There is no fixed order for frying the vegetables, and it is left up to the personal preferences of the guests.

450 g (1 lb) lean beef, very thinly sliced
2 medium aubergines, halved lengthwise and sliced crosswise
2 medium onions, halved and sliced
2 medium green peppers, de-seeded and cut into 2.5 cm (1 in) strips
225 g (8 oz) mushrooms, sliced
4 tablespoons vegetable oil

SAUCE

100 ml (4 fl oz) soy sauce
225 ml (8 fl oz) water or soup stock
3 tablespoons sugar
2 tablespoons mirin or sweet sherry

Arrange meat and vegetables on a large serving dish and lay at the table adjacent to a hot plate. Combine sauce ingredients and distribute sauce among four small bowls. Heat half the oil in a heavy frying pan over a hot plate. The guests, using chopsticks, now dip a piece of food into their bowl of sauce, drop it into the frying pan, fry it, and dip it again into the sauce before eating it. Add more oil as it is needed and replenish bowls of dipping sauce if they get low.

Chicken Sukiyaki

225 ml (8 fl oz) chicken stock
3 tablespoons sugar
4 tablespoons soy sauce
450 g (1 lb) boned chicken, thinly sliced
2 medium carrots, parboiled and sliced diagonally
1 medium onion, sliced thinly
1 medium green pepper, cut into 1.25 cm (1 in) wide strips
1 medium lettuce, chopped coarsely
350 g (12 oz) tofu, cut into 2.5 cm (1 in) cubes (optional)
100 g (4 oz) mushrooms, left whole
4 eggs
2 tablespoons vegetable oil

Combine the first three ingredients, mix well and transfer the sauce to a jug. Arrange the remaining ingredients, except oil, on one or two large serving dishes and place on the table, together with the sauce, alongside the hot plate. Heat oil in a heavy frying pan and add half the chicken; lightly brown both sides. Push chicken to one side, add half the onions and green pepper, lightly fry before adding half the carrots, lettuce, tofu and mushrooms. Pour in two-thirds of the sauce and cook until vegetables are tender. Meanwhile, invite each guest to break an egg into a small bowl and to lightly whisk it with chopsticks. The guests may now begin to help themselves, with their chopsticks, to the cooked food, which is dipped into the egg before being eaten. When the first helping is finished, replenish the pan with uncooked ingredients and the remaining sauce.

Lemon juice may be used in place of raw egg as a dipping sauce, and if you wish, season the cooking food with 7-spices pepper or cayenne.

Fish Sukiyaki

850 ml (1½ pt) fish stock (prepare from head and bones of
fish)
4 tablespoons sake or white wine or dry sherry
9 large Chinese cabbage leaves
225 g (8 oz) spinach
450 ml (1 pt) water, plus a pinch of salt
450 g (1 lb) filleted fish, thinly sliced (cod, hake, salmon,
mackerel, etc.)
2 tablespoons vegetable oil
25 g (1 oz) ginger root, grated
Juice of 1 lemon
4 tablespoons soy sauce
2 leeks or 6 spring onions, cut into 3.75 cm (1½ in) lengths
2 bamboo shoots, thinly sliced
350 g (12 oz) tofu, cut into 2.5 cm (1 in) cubes

Combine fish stock, sugar and sake, mix well and transfer
the sauce to a jug. Heat salted water to boiling and lightly
parboil Chinese cabbage leaves for 30 seconds to one
minute. Lift from pot and rinse under cold water. Drain.
Collect spinach leaves with stems all at one end. Return
salted water to the boil and holding small bunch of spinach
by the stems dip into the water for 30 seconds to one minute.
Rinse under cold water and drain. Arrange three cabbage
leaves with stems and leaves alternately overlapping on a
sudare (bamboo mat) or thick moist cloth. Lay a third of the
spinach leaves horizontally across the centre, alternating
leaves and stems. Roll cabbage leaves and spinach into tight
bundles, remove sudare or cloth, and cut into 2.5 cm (1 in)
lengths. Mix ginger, lemon juice and soy sauce and place in a
small bowl. Arrange cabbage rolls and remaining ingredients on one or two large serving dishes and lay on the table
with sauce and ginger or lemon mixture. Set the hot plate to
medium, and heat the oil in a heavy frying pan. Add the fish,

lightly fry both sides and then add half the vegetables and half the tofu. Pour over two-thirds of the sauce and cook until vegetables are tender. The guests may now help themselves to cooked food. Dip into ginger/lemon mixture before eating. Replenish pan with remaining vegetables and tofu as required. Watercress may be used in place of spinach in preparation of cabbage rolls.

Mizutaki

The arrangements for this dish are similar to those for sukiyaki, but the food is boiled in soup stock, not fried. In some of the recipes the ingredients are partially cooked in the kitchen and finished off at the table. Side dishes that customarily accompany mizutaki are boiled rice, grated fresh ginger root, finely minced spring onion or leek plus seasoning and large amounts of green tea and sake.

Beef Mizutaki

2 l (3½ pt) soup stock
450 g (1 lb) lean beef, very thinly sliced
225 g (8 oz) mushrooms, sliced
1 small cauliflower, cut into flowerettes
225 g (8 oz) Chinese or white cabbage, coarsely chopped
2 medium green peppers, cut into 1.25 cm (½ in) wide strips
2 leeks or 6 spring onions cut into 3.75 cm (1½ in) lengths
350 g (12 oz) tofu, cut into 2.5 cm (1 in) cubes
4 eggs (optional)

EGG SAUCE
225 ml (8 fl oz) soy sauce
1 egg, beaten
2 cloves garlic, crushed

SESAME SAUCE
    50 g (2 oz) sesame seeds, toasted
    225 ml (8 fl oz) soup stock
    ½ teaspoon hot pepper sauce

RELISHES FOR MIZUTAKI
    4 tablespoons spring onion, minced
    50 g (2 oz) ginger root, grated
    Salt and togarashi or black pepper

On a stove in the kitchen, bring the soup stock to the boil in a
heat-proof casserole. At the table, adjust hot plate to
medium heat and transfer the casserole to it. Arrange
remaining ingredients on one or two serving dishes and lay
alongside hot plate. Combine ingredients of one or both
sauces and serve each guest with a separate bowl of sauce.
Invite each guest to add a selection of beef and vegetable
pieces to the pot. Simmer for five minutes and then add part
of the tofu and spinach. Heat through, and the guests may
now help themselves to the cooked food, dipping it into the
sauce and relishes before eating. Replenish the pot as it
empties. Towards the end of the meal break one egg per
guest into the simmering broth and poach. Remove to bowls
with a slotted spoon and ladle out the remaining stock over
the poached egg. Sip the liquid directly from the bowl after
finishing off the egg.

Other additional vegetable suggestions for this dish, as
well as for the Chicken Mizutaki recipe that follows, are:

Celery, cut into 2.5 cm (1 in) lengths
Fresh asparagus, cut into 2.5 cm (1 in) lengths
Broccoli flowerettes
Watercress
Bamboo shoots, thinly sliced
Water chestnuts, thinly sliced
Lotus roots, thinly sliced

French beans, stringed, cut into 5 cm (2 in) lengths
Peas in the pod
Shiitake, soaked

Chicken Mizutaki

The chicken is cut into small pieces, boiled and the chicken
plus cooking liquid are then brought to the table where the
other ingredients are cooked in the same pot.

1–1½ kg (2–3 lbs) chicken
1.75 l (3 pt) water
5 cm (2 in) square kombu, washed (optional)
2 stalks celery, cut into 2.5 cm (1 in) lengths
4 shiitake or 4 large mushrooms, stems removed
225 g (8 oz) spinach or watercress

SAUCE
100 ml (4 fl oz) soy sauce
Juice of 2 lemons
1 tablespoon mirin or sherry (optional)

GARNISHES
As for Beef Mizutaki

Cut chicken, including skin and bones into several pieces,
add to the water in a heat-proof casserole or large pan and
bring the water to the boil. Continue boiling while scum rises
to the surface, scooping it off as it forms, then reduce heat,
cover and simmer for 40–50 minutes or until chicken is
tender. Meanwhile, arrange remaining ingredients on a large
serving dish and transfer to the table. Combine sauce
ingredients and give each guest a small bowl of sauce. Lay
out small dishes of garnishes. Set hot plate to high and
transfer casserole to it, add kombu and the other vegetables
and cook until tender. Remove the kombu and discard.

Invite guests to help themselves to pieces of chicken and vegetables, dipping into sauce and garnishing before eating. When all the chicken and vegetables have been eaten, ladle out the cooking broth and drink straight from the bowl.

Fish Mizutaki

450 g (1 lb) filleted white fish and/or 450 g (1 lb) prawns, shelled and deveined

2 medium carrots, parboiled, cut into 2.5 cm (1 in) lengths

450 g (1 lb) potatoes, peeled, cut into 0.5 cm ($\frac{1}{4}$ in) thick slices

2 leeks or 6 spring onions, cut into 5 cm (2 in) lengths

100 g (4 oz) somen or vermicelli noodles, cut into 10 cm (4 in) lengths

1 teaspoon salt

7.5 cm (3 in) piece of kombu, washed (optional)

865 ml (1$\frac{1}{2}$ pt) soup stock

DIPPING SAUCE
See Beef Mizutake dipping sauces (page 154–5)

Arrange the fish, prawns, carrots, potatoes, leeks and noodles on a serving dish and lay on the table. Sprinkle fish and prawns with salt. On an oven in the kitchen bring soup stock to the boil in a heat-proof casserole or large pan. Add kombu, transfer to the table and set on hot plate to simmer. Invite guests to select and add ingredients to the pot. Cook for a minute or two, remove, dip into sauce and eat. At the end of the meal ladle out any left-over stock and drink directly from the bowl.

Shabu-Shabu

Similar to mizutaki, but instead of dropping the ingredients into the cooking stock, they are held in chopsticks and moved about in the simmering broth. The name derives from the noise made as the food is swished about.

> Juice of 1 lemon
> 2 tablespoons wasabi or English mustard paste
> 1 l (2 pt) soup stock
> 7.5 cm (3 in) piece of kombu (optional)
> 700 g ($1\frac{1}{2}$ lb) lean beef, very thinly sliced
> 2–3 leeks or 6 spring onions, cut into 5 cm (2 in) lengths
> 350 g (12 oz) small mushrooms, halved
> 350 g (12 oz) tofu, cut into 2.5 cm (1 in) cubes (optional)
> 225 g (8 oz) Chinese or white cabbage and/or 225 g (8 oz)
> 　　spinach, coarsely chopped

DIPPING SAUCE
See Beef Mizutaki (p. 154–5)

Serve dipping sauce in small individual bowls and lemon juice and wasabi in small central bowls. Bring soup stock to the boil in heat-proof casserole in the kitchen. Now set to simmer on hot plate at the table. Add kombu. Arrange remaining ingredients on serving dish and bring to the table. Invite guests to adjust their dipping sauce to taste with lemon juice and wasabi. Now, using chopsticks, select a piece of beef or vegetable and swish it around in the simmering stock. Do not overcook the meat; it tastes best when dark pink to pale brown in colour. Dip cooked morsel into sauce and eat. When all the meat and vegetables are eaten, ladle the cooking liquid out and drink directly from the bowls. Discard kombu.

Chinese Cabbage Nabe

This is a basic recipe. For a more elaborate dish use some of the variations suggested below.

4 shiitake or 100 g (4 oz) mushrooms, sliced
450 g (1 lb) Chinese cabbage
1 l (2 pt) water
Pinch of salt
2 tablespoons vegetable oil
1 medium onion, diced
100 g (4 oz) tomatoes, sliced
1 medium carrot, sliced, parboiled in a little salted water
850 ml (1½ pt) soup stock
175 g (6 oz) tofu cut into 2.5 cm (1 in) cubes
Soy sauce and 7-spices pepper or cayenne to taste

Soak mushrooms in cold water for 20 minutes. Drain, remove hard stems and thinly slice. Bring water to boil, salt. Separate cabbage leaves and, holding leaf part, dip stems into boiling water until just soft. Now hold stems and momentarily dip green leaf part into the water. Rinse in cold water and drain. Arrange three cabbage leaves alternately, with stems and leaves overlapping, on a sudare (bamboo mat) or thick cloth. Roll up into a tight bundle. Squeeze, remove sudare or cloth and cut into 2.5 cm (1 in) lengths. Repeat for all the cabbage leaves. Arrange all the ingredients on large serving dishes and set on table around hot plate. Set heavy deep frying pan on hot plate adjusted to high heat, add oil, heat and then add onions and mushrooms and fry quickly. Add tomatoes and pour in soup stock. Bring to the boil, add carrots, cabbage rolls and gently boil for ten minutes. Add tofu, season with soy sauce and 7-spices pepper. Invite guests to help themselves to cooked food. Finally, ladle out remaining stock and drink straight from the bowl. Any of the dipping sauces given in previous recipes may be served with this dish.

Variations on the above recipe. The tofu can be grilled before use to give it extra colour and texture. Pre-heat high grill. Place cake of tofu in shallow dish and add water to come halfway up the sides of the tofu. Place dish under grill and toast top of tofu for a few seconds. As soon as it is speckled brown, turn it over and repeat on the other side.

To add meat to the dish, sauté 350 g (12 oz) of minced beef or pork along with the onions and mushrooms; that is, add the meat before adding the stock.

Add seasonal vegetables as available.

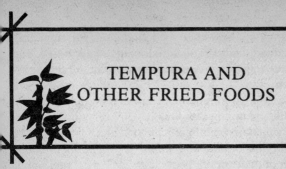

TEMPURA AND OTHER FRIED FOODS

Tempura is made by dipping pieces of food, usually fish, shellfish or vegetables in a batter, deep frying and serving with a special tempura dipping sauce. It is quite rightly one of Japan's most famous dishes. It sounds simple to prepare but, to produce crispy, light tempura, care is necessary. The essence of success is freshness. The batter is made immediately before use. The food to be coated with batter should be fresh and newly cleaned and cut and the oil for deep frying must also be clean. Ideally, the tempura should be eaten immediately after cooking. In Japanese restaurants that specialize in tempura, the chef stands in view of the customer while he deep fries the selected foods. Afterwards he quickly arranges them on a paper-covered bamboo basket and hands them across the counter to the customer, hot, crisp and full of flavour. This immediacy is not possible if you are making tempura at home for four or five people, so either you can store the cooked tempura in a pre-heated oven at 120°C (250°F) until they are all prepared or sit in the kitchen area and take turns with your guests in making tempura for one another. I have, in fact, been given cold tempura as part of a lunchtime snack; it wasn't too bad, so if you make too much, use it later.

For deep frying the tempura, vegetable oil should be used since animal fat makes it soggy. The addition of one-third or more sesame seed oil will give the tempura a pleasing nutty taste. After use strain the oil and store in a sealed bottle. The Japanese put an umeboshi plum in with the oil to keep it extra fresh.

The procedure for preparing tempura is given in the order you should follow when making it. The recipe for tempura sauce is given first, followed by the preparation of the ingredients and batter, and finally the method for deep frying. Serve the tempura with plain, hot boiled rice, and, if you wish, a crisp green salad.

Tempura Sauces

Tentsuyu

This is the traditional sauce for tempura. Grated daikon and ginger root are either combined with the sauce or served alongside in small separate containers. Daikon aids the digestion of oils and is a very suitable accompaniment. If you cannot obtain any, substitute small white turnips.

225 ml (8 fl oz) dashi, soup stock or water
50 ml (2 fl oz) soy sauce
50 ml (2 fl oz) mirin or sweet sherry
100 g (4 oz) daikon, grated
50 g (2 oz) ginger root, grated

Combine dashi, soy sauce and mirin and bring to the boil. Cool and divide amongst four bowls. Add a portion of daikon and ginger to each.

Lemon and Salt

This is a simpler accompaniment than tentsuyu. Simply quarter two lemons, distribute among four small dishes, mound a little salt in each dish and give one to each guest.

Squeeze lemon juice on to tempura, dip into salt, and eat.

Salt or Soy Sauce

Easiest of all is to just sprinkle tempura with soy sauce or salt.

Tempura Ingredients

Many varieties of foods can be used in the preparation of tempura and there are no fixed rules for dictating what ingredients to use. The limits are set by personal choice, imagination and availability. Below is a list of recommended vegetables and seafoods and details of how to prepare them for tempura cooking. Amounts are not given; these will, of course, depend on how many are being catered for and how much of any one ingredient you wish to use. From my own experience, tempura is eaten heartily and a rough guide for a full meal would be 350 g (12 oz) of vegetable (total) and the same amount of seafood per person.

Vegetable Tempura

Artichoke hearts

Asparagus, cut in 2.5 cm (1 in) diagonal slices

Aubergines, cut in 0.5 cm (¼ in) thick slices cut in half. Alternatively, cut aubergine in half lengthwise. Now cut each half vertically into four or five slices, but leave root end up to depth of 3.75 cm (1½ in) intact. You end up with a sort of aubergine fan.

Bamboo shoots, 1.25 cm (½ in) thick slices, cut into half moons.

Broccoli, separated into flowerettes

Carrots, 0.25 cm (⅛ in) thick, flower-shaped slices or matchsticks.

Cauliflower, separated into flowerettes.

Celery, 0.5 cm (¼ in) thick, diagonal slices.

Chestnuts, boiled and peeled.

French beans, cut into 5 cm (2 in) lengths

Green peppers, de-seeded, quartered lengthwise.

Leeks, 2.5–5 cm (1 in–2 in) lengths.

Lotus root, 1.25 cm (½ in) thick rounds.

Mushrooms, use whole if small, otherwise sliced.

Nuts, use whole almonds, cashews, hazels or walnuts.

Onions, 1.25 cm (½ in) thick rounds.

Parsley, sprigs drawn together in small bunches.

Parsnips, 1.25 cm (½ in) thick rounds or matchsticks.

Peas in the pod.

Potatoes, 1.25 cm (½ in) thick rounds, halved if large.

Pumpkin, peeled, de-seeded, cut into 2.5 cm (1 in) cubes.

Shiitake, washed in cold water for 20 minutes, hard stems cut off, drained. Batter on top side only.

Spinach, cut away some stem, sprinkle with flour before battering.

Spring onions, cut into 2.5-5 cm (1 in-2 in) lengths, green part as well.

Squash, as for pumpkin.

Tofu, pressed and cut into 2.5 cm (1 in) cubes.

Turnips, 1.25 cm (½ in) thick slices, quartered.

Watercress in small bunches, lightly floured before battering.

Seafood Tempura

Prawns, shell and devein.

Shrimps, shell and devein, score two or three incisions across the inside curve of the body and press flat with broad side of a knife. This prevents the shrimp curling during cooking.

Fish, cut filleted pieces into bite-size amounts. Leave small fish whole. For fish a little bigger than, say, whitebait, fillet first but then leave whole.

Mussels, wash, boil, remove shells and cut in half if large.
Crab or lobster, shell and cut into slices.
Nori seaweed, cut 1 sheet into eight pieces.
Kombu seaweed, cut into thin strips, put two together and
   tie into a knot.
Slices or cubes of cooked meat or poultry may also be used to
   make tempura.

Batter for Tempura

The batter is intended for use immediately after preparation,
and it does not matter if it contains a few lumps. It is a good
idea to mix the batter while the deep frying oil is heating up.

   100 g (4 oz) plain flour
   1 egg
   275 ml (10 fl oz) water

Combine ingredients together and whisk lightly or do as the
Japanese do and use the blunt end of a chopstick for mixing.
Do not stir again having once mixed the batter. For variety
try different types of flour, e.g. wholewheat, rye, buckwheat,
etc., or combinations of these.

Deep Frying Method for Tempura

Pour vegetable oil 5–7.5 cm (2 in–3 in) deep into a deep
frying pan. Start heating the oil and meanwhile prepare
batter. Heat the oil to 160°–175°C (320°–350°F), and
maintain at this temperature. At 175°C (350°F) a small lump
of batter dropped into the oil will cook golden brown in one
minute. Using a pair of chopsticks, pick up one piece of food
(fry strong tasting foods, such as fish, last), dip it into the
batter, shake off excess, and drop coated food into the oil.
Do not fry too much at once. Turn food once during cooking
if it looks necessary. Allow it to crisp and brown. Remove
from oil, shake off excess fat, and set to drain on absorbent

paper. Once the first batch is cooked, remove any floating pieces of batter from the oil, and then fry another portion. Keep the oil at the right temperature since if it gets too low, the food starts to absorb the oil and you will get soggy tempura.

If you are planning to prepare a lot of tempura, pre-heat a moderate oven and store the cooked tempura until you have finished all the ingredients. Now cover the bottom of a bamboo or wicker basket with soft paper, arrange the tempura on top and serve with dipping sauce and boiled rice as described.

Tempura and Other Fried Dishes

Chicken Tempura

> 4 chicken breasts, skinned and boned.
> 1 l (2 pt) water
> Salt and black pepper to taste
> Tempura Sauces and Batter

Cut chicken breasts into four pieces. Bring water to the boil and drop in the pieces. Boil for one minute. Remove, drain and season with salt and black pepper. Prepare batter and deep fry coated chicken as described above.

Vegetable Dumpling Tempura (Kakiage)

In kakiage dishes, the tempura batter is mixed with the other ingredients and not used as a coating. Serve as for ordinary tempura.

100 g (4 oz) plain wholemeal flour
Pinch of salt
225–275 ml (8–10 fl oz) water
100 g (4 oz) sweet corn (tinned)
1 medium carrot, grated
1 medium onion, finely diced
1 lotus root, thinly sliced and quartered (optional)
Oil for deep frying

Combine the flour, salt and enough water to form a stiff batter. Add the vegetables and stir thoroughly. Heat the oil to 175°C (350°F) and drop in tablespoonfuls of batter and vegetables. Fry until golden brown and crisp (about one minute). Other vegetables, pieces of fish, shellfish or meat may be added to or replace the vegetables suggested.

Tempura Tendon

A favourite Japanese restaurant dish is tendon, which is simply a bowl of steaming hot, boiled rice, topped with pieces of tempura and dressed with tempura sauce.

Tempura Soba

As for tempura tendon, but the rice is replaced by a bowl of soba noodles.

Japanese Pancakes (Okonomi-Yaki)

One of my most enjoyable restaurant meals in Japan was in a 'cook-it-yourself' pancake house in Tokyo. The restaurant was on the eighth floor of a ten-storey building, and on each level there were numerous other restaurants, each specializing in a particular type of cooking. The pancake place was lined with low tables, each inset with a large hot plate. Each diner was given a large bowl containing a bottom layer of pancake mixture, followed by a layer of vegetables and fish and topped with a raw egg.

We seasoned our bowls of food with a variety of sauces, mixed it all together and then proceeded to fry portions on the hot plate. We cooked delicious pancakes, each custom made. Finally, as a last course we were served a huge tray of cooked noodles and fresh vegetables to fry.

You may wish to prepare these pancakes in the manner described in the chapter on table-cooked meals, but otherwise cook them in the kitchen and keep them warm in a pre-heated moderate oven until you are ready to serve.

75 g (3 oz) plain flour
75 g (3 oz) water
3 eggs
1 teaspoon soy sauce

Plus a selection of five of the following:

½ medium onion, diced
50 g (2 oz) cabbage, shredded
50 g (2 oz) mushrooms, sliced
½ medium carrot, cut into matchsticks
1 small green pepper, diced
50 g (2 oz) French beans, cut into 5 cm (2 in) lengths
50 g (2 oz) sweetcorn (tinned)
50 g (2 oz) shelled and parboiled or tinned peas
100 g (4 oz) tofu, mashed
100 g (4 oz) white fish, flaked
100 g (4 oz) cooked chicken, diced
100 g (4 oz) cooked beef or pork, diced
4 prawns or shrimps, shelled and deveined
2 tablespoons vegetable oil

Combine the first four ingredients into a smooth batter. Add your selected combination of other ingredients and mix well. Heat half the oil in a heavy frying pan and ladle in a portion of the mixture. Cook on both sides over a low heat. Repeat for remaining batter, adding oil as required.

Rolled Omelette (Omeretsu)

    4 eggs
    1 teaspoon soy sauce
    Pinch of ground ginger (optional)
    1 tablespoon plain flour
    1 tablespoon vegetable oil

SAUCE (*optional*)
    2 tablespoons sugar
    2 tablespoons soy sauce
    2 tablespoons fresh parsley or bonito flakes
    Togarashi or black pepper to taste

Beat the eggs and add soy sauce and ginger. Sift the flour and beat into the eggs. Heat oil in a heavy frying pan over a medium heat. Pour in the egg mixture and cook until set, gently turn it over and cook the other side. Ideally, the omelette should be 1.25 cm (½ in) thick. Remove to a plate and allow to cool. Trim the omelette into a rectangle and place on a sudare (bamboo mat) or damp cloth. Place the trimmings across the centre of the omelette and roll it up into a cylinder. Remove the cloth or sudare and slice into 2.5 cm (1 in) thick rolls. Pour over sauce if desired.

SWEETS
AND CAKES

The Japanese are not great dessert eaters and there is no set custom that a meal should be followed by something sweet. The normal manner of ending a meal is to serve fresh fruit, carefully washed and cut into segments. However, during the day or late evening, when friends may visit to chat over a pot of tea, sweets and cakes are eaten. They are also made for festival times and other celebrations. Little cakes, called manju, that look like dumplings are prepared from sweet bean jam, flour and water.

Jellied sweets are made from fruit, sugar and kanten (also called agar-agar), a sort of gelatine, and other sweets are made simply from eggs, colouring and sugar. In fact, most of the cakes and sweets are made from simple ingredients, and the differences between them are emphasized more by the way the ingredients are combined and cooked than by their variety. The basic headings under which this chapter is arranged are: bean jam cakes and desserts, yokan (jellied) sweets and sweets containing eggs.

Bean Jam Cakes and Desserts

Bean Jam

This is used as a filling or as a coating around other fillings and is usually made from aduki beans, but red kidney beans can be used just as effectively. For white jam, haricot beans are substituted. The jam is prepared by two methods. Which method is chosen depends on the texture of the jam required. For smooth jam, the beans are boiled soft, rubbed through a sieve or strainer and then puréed with sugar. For a coarser jam, the beans are boiled soft, mashed with sugar and boiled to remove excess water. The same quantities of ingredients are used in both cases. The recipe that follows makes twice as much jam as will be required for subsequent cake recipes. The unused jam, if stored in a glass jar with a tight lid, will keep indefinitely.

450 g (1 lb) aduki beans
Water
2 teaspoons salt
450 g (1 lb) sugar

Wash the beans, transfer to a heavy pan, add just enough water to cover and boil until the beans are soft and the shells have started to peel off (about one hour). If you substitute red kidney or haricot beans for aduki beans, soak them for six to eight hours before use. Proceed by one of the following methods.

Smooth Bean Jam

Drain the beans, force them through a sieve or fine colander, place the pulp in a clean towel or piece of cheesecloth and squeeze out any remaining liquid. Return pulp to pan, add salt, and over a low heat gradually stir in the sugar. Continue heating, stirring and cook down to form a stiff smooth mixture.

Coarse Bean Jam

Add salt and sugar to the soft boiled beans and reduce over a low heat. Mash to a paste with a wooden spoon.

Manju

Small dumplings or cakes made by steaming balls of bean jam wrapped in a flour dough.

350 g (12 oz) flour
2 teaspoons baking powder
225 g (8 oz) sugar
225 ml (8 fl oz) water
Pinch of salt
450 g (1 lb) bean jam

Sift the flour and baking powder together. Dissolve the sugar in the water, add a pinch of salt and stir in the flour mixture to form a smooth dough. Roll the dough into a thin sheet and cut into 16–20 10 cm (4 in) squares. Form the bean paste into the same number of balls as there are wrappings, and wrap each one. Pinch the sides of dough squares together, and place the dumplings seam side down on a wet towel in a steamer (see pp. 17–18). Steam for 20 minutes over a medium heat. Cool and serve.

The manju can also be given a Western touch by baking them instead of steaming. Place the formed uncooked dumplings on a greased baking tray, brush with egg yolk and bake in a pre-heated oven at 190°C (375°F) for 20 minutes. I have tried making manju using brown flour, and it works if you bake them, but it makes the steamed variety very heavy.

To add flavour and colourings to the dumplings, add a teaspoon or two of cinnamon or green tea powder to the flour. Chestnut purée may also be used in place of bean jam or try a mixture of the two.

Roly Poly Manju

Use same ingredients as for manju recipe above. Prepare the dough as for manju, divide it into two, and roll each half into a rectangular sheet. Spread each with bean jam and roll up into a cylinder. Steam or bake as for manju recipe. Cool, cut into slices and serve.

Rice Cakes with Sweet Bean Soup (Shiruko)

Bean soup with lightly fried rice cakes, even if it is sweet, sounds a strange dessert to Western ears, but the Japanese really do have a different idea of what, where and when sweet things should be served and sometimes even serve them at the beginning of a meal.

    100 g (4 oz) rice flour
    Pinch of salt
    100 ml (4 fl oz) boiling water, approximately
    1 tablespoon vegetable oil
    850 ml (1½ pt) water
    450 g (1 lb) bean jam
    1 tablespoon arrowroot (or cornflour)
    Salt to taste.

Combine rice flour with salt and slowly pour in the boiling water, mix well, adjust water to form a smooth elastic dough, and knead for one to two minutes. Pinch off bite-size pieces of dough and form into balls, then flatten them slightly. Heat oil in a heavy frying pan, add rice cakes and brown both sides. Set aside. Bring water to the boil and stir in bean jam. Dissolve arrowroot in a little boiling soup and then blend it into the main body of the soup to thicken it. Season to taste with salt. Divide rice cakes among four bowls, pour the soup over them and serve.

Rice Cakes with Bean Jam and Chestnut Cream

100 g (4 oz) rice flour
Pinch of salt
100 ml (4 fl oz) boiling water, approximately
1 tablespoon vegetable oil
225 g (8 oz) bean jam
100 g (4 oz) chestnut purée
100 g (4 oz) water

Using the first four ingredients, prepare and fry the rice cakes as described in the recipe on p. 173. Combine the bean jam, chestnut purée and water, and bring to the boil with stirring. Reduce heat and simmer. Divide rice cakes among four bowls, pour over bean jam and chestnut cream and serve.

Candied Chestnuts

450 g (1 lb) chestnuts, washed and soaked for 6–8 hours in
    450 ml (16 fl oz) water
100 g (4 oz) honey
225 g (8 oz) sugar

Drain soaked chestnuts, and reserve water. Peel chestnuts. Place reserved water, honey and sugar in a heavy pan and, over a low heat, dissolve the sugar. Add the chestnuts, cover and simmer very gently for one hour (use an asbestos pad under the pan if possible). Spoon the chestnuts separately on to a greased tray and leave to cool.

For a more elaborate sweet, coat the candied chestnuts in bean jam. Other large nuts may be substituted for chestnuts.

Jellied Sweets (Yokan)

Kanten or agar-agar is similar to gelatine, and it is used in Japanese cooking in the same way as we may use jelly (jello in America). Kanten sets at 30°C (85°F) and melts at 82°C (180°F), which means that once made it remains firm, even on the hottest day. It is sold in blocks that weigh 8 g ($\frac{1}{3}$ oz). One block is soaked in 450 ml (16 fl oz) water, boiled, strained, cooled to room temperature, and then mixed with other ingredients. As long as it is mixed when cold, it can safely be re-heated without separation from the other ingredients. Sticks of agar-agar weighing the same amount and reconstituted in the same way are available in the West. Otherwise, substitute three tablespoons gelatine for one block of kanten, and reduce the water required in the recipe by one quarter.

Red Bean Jelly Cakes (Yokan)

    1 cake kanten
    450 ml (16 fl oz) water
    225 g (8 oz) sugar (optional)
    350 ml (12 oz) bean jam
    Salt to taste

Soak kanten in water for 30 minutes, then bring to the boil and boil until kanten is dissolved. Pass solution through a strainer, return to the pan and add sugar (leave this out or reduce the amount if you do not have a very sweet tooth) and bean jam, and stir over a low heat until well blended. Season to taste with salt. Pour mixture into a small square or round cake tin and leave to set. Cut into portions and serve with green tea.

Chestnut, apple and pumpkin purées may be substituted for bean jam. For extra flavour and texture, add toasted sesame seeds and/or grated lemon peel to the jelly.

Sweet Fruit Jelly (Awayaki Kan)

> 225 g (8 oz) fresh fruit, diced
> 1 block kanten
> 450 ml (16 fl oz) water
> 100 g (4 oz) sugar
> 2 egg whites

Soak kanten in water for 30 minutes then bring to the boil and boil until kanten is dissolved. Pass solution through strainer, return to the pan and add sugar. Stir over a low heat until the mixture gets stringy when a spoonful is held in the air. Cool to below 37°C (100°F). Beat the egg whites stiff in a large bowl and add the kanten mixture, slowly stirring all the time. Wet the inside surface of a square mould or cake tin and arrange a bottom layer of fruit. Pour over the egg white and kanten mixture. Chill and serve.

An alternative way of preparing jellied fruit is to flavour the dissolved kanten with vanilla or peppermint or other extracts, pour it into a mould and allow to set. Decorate the jelly with fresh fruit and serve.

Tangerine Bags

The Girls' Festival is celebrated on the 3rd of March, and special dishes are made for the children. At the same time of the year tangerines are in great abundance, and the two events are celebrated in this lovely sweet.

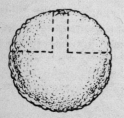

4 tangerines
225 g (8 oz) water
½ cake kanten
50 g (2 oz) sugar

Cut the tangerine as shown, and remove the flesh from the inside. Squeeze the juice from the flesh and add to the water. Soak the kanten in this mixture for 30 minutes. Then bring to the boil and boil until kanten is dissolved. Pass through a strainer, add sugar, simmer over a low heat until dissolved. Cool and, just before jelly sets, spoon into the tangerine shells, chill and serve.

Sweets Containing Eggs

Sweet Hard Boiled Eggs (Nishiki Tamago)

6 hard boiled eggs
100 g (4 oz) sugar
Pinch of salt

Shell eggs and separate yolks from whites. Mash each with a fork. Separately combine yolk and half the sugar, and the egg white, remaining sugar and salt. In the bottom of a small round or square cake tin (15 cm × 15 cm, 6 in × 6 in approximately), press the egg white mixture into an even layer. Spread the yolk mixture on top and lightly press down. Steam tin for 10 minutes over a moderate heat, or bake in a pre-heated oven at 175°C (350°F) for 10 minutes. Cool, cut into squares and serve.

For two-coloured sandwiches, layer half the egg white mixture in the bottom of the cake tin. Cover with all the egg yolk mixture and top with remaining egg white.

A more elaborate way of preparing nishiki tamago is in the shape of a flower petal. Spread a piece of damp cheesecloth 25 cm (10 in) square on a sudare or bamboo

place mat. Spread the egg white mixture over it. Layer
horizontally across the middle a line of the egg yolk mixture.
Roll up into a cylinder and remove the sudare, leaving the
cheesecloth in place. Now arrange five chopsticks equally
around the cylinder and while you hold them in place, get
somebody else to tie them tightly into position. The finished
job looks like a rolled cylinder with five splints. Steam the
whole thing (a fish kettle is excellent for this job). Remove
the chopsticks, which leaves five equally spaced indentations
in the egg roll, and the cheesecloth and cut the roll into 1.25
cm ($\frac{1}{2}$ in) thick slices. For extra colour, dye the egg white
with food colouring.

Fruit Tempura

Fresh fruit for four people (apple, pear, banana, etc.)
Tempura batter (see p. 165)
Oil for deep frying
4 tablespoons honey

Peel and cut up fruit into mouth-sized pieces. Prepare
tempura batter and proceed to batter and deep fry the fruit in
the way described in the chapter on Tempura (see pp. 165–6).
Divide the fruit tempura among four bowls, pour over honey
and serve.

Stuffed Pancakes

Pancakes stuffed with bean jam or with a sweet miso and
lemon filling called nerimiso.

PANCAKE BATTER
225 g (8 oz) flour, white or wholemeal
275 ml (10 fl oz) water
1 egg, lightly beaten
2 teaspoons rice flour
2 tablespoons vegetable oil

Combine the first four ingredients of the pancake batter, and mix to a smooth paste. Lightly oil a heavy frying pan and prepare 12–16 thin pancakes. Re-oil the pan as needed. Spoon filling on to each pancake, roll up and serve.

FILLINGS
   350 g (12 oz) bean jam (see pp. 170–1)
   or
NERIMISO FILLING
   225 g (8 oz) miso (white is best)
   2 tablespoons sugar
   1 tablespoon water
   Rind of 1 lemon, grated

Combine all the ingredients of nerimiso filling, bring to the boil, reduce heat and simmer for two to three minutes. Remove from heat.

Fried Ball Cake (Sata Tempura)

This is a famous Okinawan cake. It is made at celebration times, and especially for engagements.

   350 g (12 oz) flour
   2 teaspoons baking powder
   225 g (8 oz) sugar
   3 eggs
   100 g (4 oz) peanuts, chopped
   3 tablespoons vegetable oil

Combine flour and baking powder. Mix sugar and egg together and add flour mixture. Stir in peanuts and one tablespoon of oil. Mix well, cover bowl with damp cloth and leave for 30 minutes. Form dough into 2.5 cm–5 cm (1 in–2 in) diameter balls. Heat remaining oil in a heavy frying pan over moderate heat. Fry the balls, turning when necessary to brown evenly all over.

   Also see dessert section of **Macrobiotic Cooking** chapter.

TEA AND BEVERAGES

Tea

The Japanese, believe it or not, are greater tea drinkers than the English. Tea, called 'cha' in Japanese, is always given the honourable prefix 'o' and called o-cha. The Japanese mainly drink green tea; it comes from the same type of plant as black tea, but it is neither dyed nor fermented. The fresh leaves are merely dried and crumbled or powdered. Various grades of green tea are available, and the quality depends on where the tea bush was grown, and from where on the bush the leaves were picked. Young, tender leaves from the top of the bush make the best teas, and the quality gets poorer as the picker moves down the bush. Bancha is the cheapest tea. It is prepared from the leaves and stems left on the plant after the more tender leaves have been picked. To make bancha tea, pour briskly boiling water over the tea (2 teaspoons per 575 ml (1 pt) water) and leave to brew for two to three minutes. Do not make it too strong or it goes bitter. All teas are drunk unsweetened without milk.

The more expensive teas are made with non-boiling water. Thus Gyokuro tea, the best and most expensive leaf tea, is made with water at 70°C (160°F). The water is poured over the tea (4 tablespoons tea per 575 ml (1 pt) water) and left to brew for five minutes. This makes a strong tea excellent with cakes in the afternoon. Green powdered tea called matcha, is the finest tea of all, and is used for the tea ceremony.

There is much ritual and skill needed to make matcha in the correct way, and it is beyond the scope of this book to go into it here. For a good book on Japanese 'teaism', and the place of tea in the Japanese culture, I would recommend an excellent one by Kakuzo Okakura called *The Book of Tea*, published in the United Kingdom by Constable & Co Ltd, and in the United States by Dover Publications Inc.

Grain tea, particularly mugicha or barley tea, is also popular in Japan. For mugicha, unhulled dry roasted barley is simmered in boiling water for five minutes. The tea is passed through a strainer before drinking. Drink hot or chilled in the summer.

Because Japanese teas are neither dyed nor fermented, they tend to be more refreshing than black teas. Tea is drunk from small cups. They are never filled more than half full, but are constantly replenished from the pot. Boiling water may be poured over the same leaves two or three times before they are discarded. In the summer chilled or iced tea is delicious and very thirst quenching.

Sake

Sake is made from fermented rice, and is probably the most popular alcoholic drink in Japan (although I think Scotch whisky, if it was cheaper, would fight a strong battle for that title). The name is said to derive from the name of Osaka, which has been the centre of sake production for many centuries. It is used in many ceremonies, particularly Shinto festivals, and rituals, and is very much part of the Japanese culture.

Sake is a little stronger than grape wine, but since it is often served warm, some of the alcohol is lost by evaporation. Not that it isn't still possible to get merry, surprisingly quickly, drinking warm sake. I found it refreshing (not because I'm a drunkard, I should add) that in

Japan no shame is attached to being a little drunk, and consequently those who had drunk a bit too much seemed less aggressive and defensive than their Western counterparts, brought up in a society more critical of drink.

The quality of sake, like whisky, depends on the water from which it was made, and the famous breweries are usually situated over or near a source of pure spring water.

Sake is served in a small thin-necked sake jug. For warm sake, the filled jug is placed in a pan of hot water up to the same level as the jug neck. The water is brought gently to the boil, the heat switched off, and the jug allowed to stand for five minutes in the water before being served. Sake should be drunk from tiny cups; Japanese tea cups will do or liqueur glasses.

Beer
Japanese beer is as good as any in the world, and if you can obtain some I recommend you to buy a bottle or two.

Japanese Whisky
Japanese whisky is quite good, but even after many years of analysing Scotch whiskies, they have still not found the secret of making the very best whisky. Johnny Walker Scotch whisky (especially Black Label) is still the best present you can give your Japanese host.

Calpis
Before the advent of coca-cola, calpis was the most popular soft drink in Japan. It is a white, milky, non-alcoholic drink that needs to be diluted with water before serving. It is served either hot or iced. The method of making calpis is closely guarded by the manufacturers, and I haven't any idea what it contains. Japanese friends told me it contains milk, but I'm not sure if they meant cow or plant milk. They were usually too busy having great fun asking me if I wanted a glass of 'cowpis' to answer serious questions.

MACROBIOTIC COOKING

The philosophy of macrobiotic cooking is based on the Chinese Yin and Yang theory of foods. The actual methods of preparation, ingredients used and cooking style of macrobiotic cooking have been developed from and are heavily influenced by traditional Japanese attitudes to food and eating. Hence the inclusion of this short chapter. I do not necessarily agree with macrobiotics, but here is a brief outline of the ideas involved.

Yin and Yang are Chinese words used to describe the intrinsic qualities of particular foods. Yin foods are said to be feminine, passive, sweet, watery, etc., while yang foods are masculine, salty, heavy, etc. The ideal is for the polarities to match. Thus a balanced diet is neither too yang nor too yin. In the summer, which is yang, a yin diet is recommended, while in the winter, the reverse is the case. The macrobiotic diet tries to balance the body's needs, and to put it in tune with its environment. Following are a number of recipes based on these principles.

Macrobiotic is not strictly vegetarian, but meat is eaten sparingly since it is considered a very yang food. Grains, particularly brown rice which is thought to be a perfectly nutritionally balanced food, are used frequently.

Apart from the recipes given here, other recipes in the book are suitable for a macrobiotic diet. The pickles and vegetable recipes are particularly suitable for accompanying the grain dishes given in this chapter.

Brown Rice
Brown rice is probably the most important part of a macrobiotic diet. Short-grain rice is considered more yang than the long variety, and boiled rice more yin than pressure-cooked rice.

Brown Rice (Boiled)

  350 g (12 oz) brown rice
  900 ml (32 fl oz) water
  Pinch of salt

Wash the rice thoroughly in cold water. Drain and transfer to a heavy pot, add the water and bring to the boil. Add a pinch of salt, cover, reduce heat and simmer for 50 minutes. Remove from heat and allow to stand for 10 minutes. Mix gently with a wooden spoon or rice paddle and serve.

Brown Rice (Pressure Cooked)

  350 g (12 oz) brown rice
  700 ml (24 fl oz) water
  Pinch of salt

Wash the rice thoroughly in cold water. Drain and transfer to a pressure cooker. Cover and bring to full pressure over a high heat. Reduce heat to very low and gently simmer for 40 minutes. Remove from heat, allow pressure to drop to normal, uncover pan, gently mix rice with wooden spoon or rice paddle, cover again and allow to stand for five minutes. Serve.

Brown Rice (Baked)

   350 g (12 oz) brown rice
   800 ml (28 fl oz) boiling water
   Pinch of salt or 1 tablespoon soy sauce

Pre-heat oven to 175°C (350°F). Wash the rice thoroughly in cold water and drain well. Place the rice in a heavy frying pan and dry roast over a medium heat until the rice is dry, deepened in colour and beginning to pop. Transfer to a casserole dish, add the boiling water and salt, cover and bake for 50 to 60 minutes. Mix gently with a wooden spoon or rice paddle and serve.

Fried Brown Rice with Vegetables

A wok is the best pan to use for preparing this dish, otherwise use a large heavy frying pan.

   2 tablespoons vegetable oil (sesame oil is best)
   1 medium onion, diced
   1 medium carrot, diced or slivers
   700 g (1½ lb) cooked brown rice
   2 tablespoons soy sauce

Heat the oil in the wok over a high heat, add the onions, followed by the carrots, and stir fry until they are heated through. Stir in the rice, reduce heat to medium and cook the rice and vegetables, with constant stirring, for three to four minutes. Sprinkle over the soy sauce, stir again and serve. For variety, add other root vegetables, cooked seaweed or lightly toasted nori seaweed. Garnish with sesame seeds.

Brown Rice Croquettes

Serve the croquettes with a crisp salad.

225 g (8 oz) brown rice, cooked
2 medium carrots, finely diced
1 medium onion, finely diced
Pinch of salt
100 g (4 oz) wholewheat flour
4 tablespoons vegetable oil

Place the rice in a large bowl and break up any sticky lumps with a wooden spoon. Add the vegetables and salt. Mix well and slowly stir in the flour to form a mixture stiff enough to form into croquettes. Make 12–15 croquettes from the mixture. If it sticks to your hands, oil them lightly. Heat half the oil in a heavy frying pan or wok and fry the rice cakes until brown on both sides, adding more oil as necessary.

Alternatively the croquettes can be deep fried. Heat 7.5 cm (3 in) to 10 cm (4 in) oil in a deep fryer to 175°C (350°F). Deep fry four to five croquettes at a time for three to four minutes or until golden brown. Drain on absorbent paper and serve. To make kasha croquettes replace the rice by the same amount of cooked buckwheat.

Buckwheat

Buckwheat (the pre-roasted variety called kasha is generally more easily available than plain buckwheat) is common in mountainous areas of Japan where the climate is too hardy for rice growing. Because it is grown in a cold climate, buckwheat is considered a yang grain and is normally eaten in the winter.

Whole Buckwheat

1 tablespoon sesame seed oil
350 g (12 oz) buckwheat
700 ml (1¼ pt) boiling water
Pinch of salt

Heat the oil in a heavy frying pan over a high heat. Add the buckwheat and fry, stirring constantly until each grain is separate and dry. Pour in the boiling water, add a pinch of salt. Reduce heat and cook for 15 minutes. Allow to stand for five minutes. Served with gomashio and cooked green vegetables (yin food).

Kasha Loaf

    1 tablespoon vegetable oil
    450 g (1 lb) cooked buckwheat
    225 g (8 oz) cooked brown rice
    1 medium onion, diced
    1 bunch parsley, chopped
    100 g (4 oz) Chinese cabbage *or* white cabbage, shredded
    Pinch of salt
    450 ml (16 fl oz) boiling water

Pre-heat oven to 175°C (350°F). Grease a casserole with oil. Combine in the casserole the remaining ingredients pouring in the boiling water last. Cover and bake for 40–50 minutes. Serve in slices hot or cold. To re-heat, toast or fry.

Buckwheat Stuffed Cabbage Rolls (with Apple Sauce)

    1 small white or Chinese cabbage
    225 g (8 oz) cooked buckwheat
    1 tablespoon sesame seeds, toasted
    Pinch of salt
    1 tablespoon vegetable oil
    225 ml (½ pt) soup stock (or water plus 1 tablespoon miso)
    1 medium onion, finely sliced

APPLE SAUCE
   900 g (2 lb) apples
   100 ml (4 fl oz) water
   1 tablespoon fresh mint leaves, chopped
   ½ teaspoon salt

Pre-heat oven to 149°C (300°F). Cut off the stem of the cabbage and separate the leaves. Soften them by steaming or dipping them into boiling water briefly. Mix the buckwheat, sesame seeds and pinch of salt. Place two or three tablespoons of mixture on each leaf and roll up. Lay the rolls seam side down in the bottom of an oiled casserole. Cover with onion rings and pour over the soup stock or water and miso. Cover and bake for 30 minutes. Meanwhile, prepare apple sauce. Core and cut the apples into eighths. Place them in a heavy pan, add the water and mint, cover and cook over a moderate heat for 20 minutes. Pass through a sieve to remove skins and serve with cabbage rolls.

Aduki Beans
Aduki beans are considered to be the most yang of all legumes and they are more popular in a macrobiotic diet than other beans which are considered secondary foods. They are used in both savoury and sweet dishes. They can also be cooked without pre-soaking, which makes them more convenient to use than other legumes.

Plain Aduki Beans

   225 g (8 oz) aduki beans
   7.5 cm (3 in) piece of kombu (optional)
   850 ml (1½ pt) water
   Pinch of salt

Wash beans thoroughly and drain. Place kombu (if being used) in the bottom of a heavy pan and add the beans. Pour in the water, bring to the boil, reduce heat to low, cover and simmer for one hour or until the beans are cooked. Remove lid, season with salt and serve.

For variety, stir sautéed vegetables into the beans five minutes before the end of the cooking time.

Aduki Bean Spread

This is excellent spread on slices of fresh bread or toast. Garnish with chopped parsley.

    2 tablespoons sesame seeds, toasted *or* 1 tablespoon tahini
    350 g (12 oz) cooked aduki beans
    Pinch of salt
    1 tablespoon sesame seed oil

Crush the sesame seeds in a suribachi or mortar. Mash the beans with a wooden spoon. Combine the beans, sesame seed paste and salt, and mix well. To heat the spread, oil a heavy frying pan, add the spread and heat through with stirring.

Baked Aduki Beans and Vegetables

    225 g (8 oz) cooked aduki beans
    2 medium carrots, diced
    2 stalks celery, chopped
    1 burdock root, thin slivers (optional)
    1 tablespoon miso
    1 tablespoon tahini
    100 ml (4 fl oz) water

Pre-heat oven to 175°C (350°F). Combine aduki beans, carrots, celery and burdock root. Mix tahini, miso and water together into a smooth paste. Transfer beans and vegetables to a casserole, stir in the paste and mix well. Cover and bake

for one hour. For variety add 25 g (1 oz) wakame or other
dried seaweed, soaked in water for ten minutes. Use part of
this water to substitute for water in recipe.

Miso

Miso is a popular macrobiotic food and because of its unique
combination of protein, vitamins, minerals and enzymes, it
is recommended as a daily food in a macrobiotic diet. Many
recipes containing miso have already been given in the book.
Below are a few Western orientated ideas on how to use
miso.

Miso Spreads

Serve in sandwiches or on toast or crackers.

Miso and Sesame Spread

> 1 tablespoon miso
> 1 tablespoon tahini
> 1 tablespoon water
> 1 tablespoon chives, chopped *or* 1 tablespoon spring
> onions, chopped *or* 1 tablespoon onion, diced *or* 1
> tablespoon watercress, chopped

Combine the first three ingredients together into a smooth
paste. Add the chives or onion, etc., and mix well. Serve. For
added tang, stir in a little grated lemon or orange peel and
one tablespoon of lemon or orange juice.

Miso and Vegetable Spread

> 2 tablespoons sesame seed oil
> 225 g (8 oz) mixed vegetables, finely chopped
> 2 tablespoons miso

Sauté a combination of vegetables in the oil. Cool, purée in a blender or pass through a sieve. Mix well with miso and serve. For extra filling, add one mashed hard boiled egg.

Miso Bread

    2 tablespoons vegetable oil
    100 g (4 oz) Brussels sprouts, quartered
    100 g (4 oz) cauliflower flowerettes
    1 medium onion, diced
    1 medium carrot, diced
    450 ml (16 fl oz) water
    2 tablespoons miso
    250 g (8 oz) wholewheat flour
    250 g (8 oz) cooked brown rice *or* buckwheat

Pre-heat oven to 175°C (350°F). Heat vegetable oil in a heavy frying pan and sauté the vegetables until soft. Combine them with the remaining ingredients and transfer to a casserole dish or bread tin. Bake for 50 minutes. Check for firmness of centre with a knife or skewer. Cook for a further ten minutes if the centre is still soft and sticky.

Miso Pâté

A good non-meat substitute for the usual chicken or pork pâté.

    100 g (4 oz) wholewheat breadcrumbs
    2 tablespoons miso
    1 medium onion, minced
    2 tablespoons parsley, chopped
    100 ml (4 fl oz) water or soup stock
    175 g (6 oz) tofu (optional)

Pre-heat oven to 175°C (350°F). Combine all the ingredients and mix into a smooth consistency. Transfer to a bread tin, gently press down to form a firm filling and bake for 45 minutes to one hour.

Desserts
Neither sugar nor honey are added to macrobiotic desserts. Instead natural sugars already present in foods are highlighted by the addition of a little salt.

Buckwheat Crêpes with Aduki Bean and Chestnut Filling

FILLING

    225 g (8 oz) aduki beans, well cooked
    100 g (4 oz) chestnut purée (or use 225 g (½ lb) fresh chestnuts, make a cut in the skins, boil for 20 minutes, peel and purée)
    1 teaspoon vanilla extract

CRÊPES

    100 g (4 oz) buckwheat flour
    Pinch of salt
    Pinch of cinnamon
    1 egg, beaten
    700 ml (1¼ pt) water
    2 tablespoons vegetable oil

Blend together aduki beans, chestnut purée and vanilla and set aside. Mix flour with salt and cinnamon, stir in the egg and then water to form a smooth batter. Heat a heavy frying pan over a moderate flame. Coat the bottom of pan with oil and pour in enough batter to just cover this area. Fry until set, turn over and brown the other side. Remove to a plate, spread with filling and fold or roll up. Set aside or store in a pre-heated oven. Repeat for remaining batter. Serve.

Aduki Bean and Apple Pie

PIE CRUST
   175 g (6 oz) wholewheat flour
   Pinch of salt
   3 tablespoons vegetable oil
   2 tablespoons sesame seeds, toasted (optional)
   575 ml (1 pt) iced water

FILLING
   225 g (8 oz) aduki beans, well cooked
   2 medium apples, peeled, cored and sliced
   1 tablespoon cinnamon
   1 egg yolk, beaten

Combine the flour, salt, oil and sesame seeds and work the
oil into the flour with your fingers. Slowly add the water to
form a firm non-sticky dough; do not use all the water if it is
not needed. Remove two-thirds of the dough and roll out on
a floured board. Line a 23 cm (9 in) pie dish. Roll out a top
from the remaining dough. Flour the top, fold it in half and
set aside. Pre-heat oven to 232°C (450°F). Mash aduki beans
and line pastry case with them. Combine apple slices and
cinnamon and layer on top of the aduki beans. Lay pastry
top over pie dish and crimp the edges with pastry lining.
Brush with egg yolk, make two cuts near the centre to let
steam escape and bake for 30 to 40 minutes.

Rice Pudding

   100 g (4 oz) brown rice
   575 ml (1 pt) water or green tea
   1 cinnamon stick
   Pinch of salt
   100 g (4 oz) raisins
   100 g (4 oz) roasted almonds

Wash the rice thoroughly. Drain. Transfer to heavy pan, add the water or tea, cinnamon stick and pinch of salt. Bring to the boil, cover and boil very gently for one hour. Pre-heat oven to 175°C (350°F). Remove cinnamon stick and transfer rice to a casserole. Stir in the raisins and almonds and bake for 25 minutes. Serve hot or cold. Alternatively, cook the rice for 90 minutes on top of the stove, then stir in the raisins and almonds, cover and allow to stand away from the heat for five minutes. Serve hot or cold.

Sesame Fingers

2 tablespoons sesame seed oil
100 ml (4 fl oz) water
100 g (4 oz) raisins
225 g (8 oz) sesame seeds
1 egg, beaten
100 g (4 oz) wholewheat flour (approximately)

Pre-heat oven to 175°C (350°F). Combine the first five ingredients. Stir in the flour to form a soft dough. Press into a greased baking tin to form a 1.25 cm (½ in) thick sheet. Bake until crisp and golden (about 30 minutes).

GLOSSARY

Some of the items listed below have already been discussed in the Ingredients chapter or elsewhere in the book, and where this is the case, only the relevant page numbers are given.

Aburage Fried Tofu, see p. 100

Aduki Beans Small red beans known as the King of Beans because they are so nutritious. They are eaten especially at festival times when their red colour represents good fortune. Mashed with sugar they are used to make bean jam, or are used as a filling in Japanese cakes.

Agar-Agar See Kanten

Bamboo Shoots (Takenoko) See p. 79

Bean Sprouts (Moyashi) See p. 80

Ben Shoga Pickled ginger root, usually dyed bright red.

Bonito Flakes (Katsuobushi) Dried fish flakes, see p. 12

Burdock Root (Gobo) See p. 83. Used as a garnishing, especially with sushi rice balls.

Chinese Cabbage (Hakusai) Crisper than lettuce and softer than white cabbage, Chinese cabbage is excellent in both salads and stews. The leaves after softening in boiling water can be wrapped around fillings, and spinach-stuffed Chinese cabbage rolls are popular in Japanese cooking.

Chrysanthemum Leaves (Shungiku) See p. 5

Daikon Japanese white radish. See p. 4

Ginger Root (Shoga) Ginger is a tropical, bamboo-like plant, with a gnarled, light brown root, about 10 cm (4 in) long. The root is peeled, and the flesh grated or chopped finely to be used for garnishing and seasoning. It is now widely available in both fresh and powdered forms. Also see p. 17

Gobo Burdock root.

Gohan White rice, cooked.

Goma Sesame seeds.

Gomashis A combination of salt and toasted sesame seeds. Grind together in a suribachi or mortar, one part sea salt with seven parts whole toasted sesame seeds.

Hakusai Chinese cabbage

Harusame Transparent noodles made from the starch of beans or vegetables (sweet potatoes in Japan). Harusame are sold dried, and need to be softened in boiling water before use. The name harusame reflects the Japanese way with descriptive titles; it means 'spring rain'.

Hijiki A black stringy seaweed sold in dried form. Rich in calcium and iron and very nutritious. See p. 1

Hocho Japanese knife, see p. 14

Kamaboko Fish cake. White fish, filleted, skinned and pounded into a paste, it is combined and cooked with cornflour and moulded into a cylinder or half-cylinder shape. Kamaboko is most popularly used in oden and other casserole dishes. Sometimes the fish is lightly coloured with pink or green dye to give coloured kamaboko.

Kanten Japanese gelatine, see p. 174

Katsuobushi Bonito flakes.

Kombu Seaweed sometimes known as sea tangle. Sold in sheets, dried. It is the main ingredient of dashi, a basic soup stock. Wipe clean before use. See p. 1

Konnyaku A gelatinous cake made from the starch of the devil's tongue plant. Used in blocks in casseroles or extruded into noodles which are known as shirataki or 'white water fall'.

Kuzu An expensive thickening starch similar to arrowroot, a suitable substitute.

Lotus Root (Renkon) See pages 5 and 89

Mirin A sweet sake wine used only for cooking. See p. 11

Miso Fermented soya bean paste. See p. 190

Moyashi Bean sprouts.

Mushrooms See shiitake, pages 5 and 91. The Japanese have many other dried mushrooms besides shiitake, but they are generally unavailable outside Japan.

Mustard Japanese mustard or powdered wasabi is hot like English mustard. Combine equal amounts of wasabi and water and blend into a smooth paste. Allow to stand for five minutes before use. One part of made-up wasabi equals one part made-up English mustard or two parts prepared horseradish paste.

Nori A purple seaweed sold in paper-thin sheets 20 cm (8 in) square. Available in Japanese stores in packets of 10 sheets. Nori is used extensively in Japanese cooking for seasoning, garnishing and wrapping other foods. See p. 1

O-cha Tea or literally 'honourable tea'.

Renkon Lotus root.

Sake Rice wine.

Sansho Pepper A spicy seasoning which also gives a brown colouring. Substitute black pepper with a pinch of sugar.

Sesame Seeds (Goma) See p. 11

Seven-Spices Pepper A hot spicy seasoning, substitute cayenne.

Shiitake Japanese tree mushrooms. See pages 5 and 91.

Shoga Ginger root.

Shoyu Soy sauce.

Shungiku Chrysanthemum leaves.

Soba Thick buckwheat noodles. See p. 57

Somen Thin wheat flour noodles. See p. 57

Soy Sauce See Shoyu

Sudare Bamboo rolling mat for wrapping foods in nori or omelette sheets. See p. 15

Suribachi Serrated mortar. See p. 15

Surikogi Pestle used with suribachi.

Takuan Pickled dried daikon.

Tofu Soy bean product. See p. 99

Togarashi Pepper See p. 12

Udon Thick wheat flour noodles. See p. 57

Umeboshi Pickled dried plum with medicinal properties. Eaten at breakfast time to aid digestion and clean the system. Added to stored foods to keep them fresh.

Wakame Sold dried in the West. Dark green, long, curly seaweed. Reconstitute in cold water and cut crosswise into short lengths. Use lightly cooked in soups or casseroles and fresh in salads.

Wasabi See Mustard.

Index

INDEX

CHINESE COOKING AND EATING FOR HEALTH
by KENNETH LO

Chinese secrets of healthy eating

Chinese cooking with its concentration on natural ingredients and careful methods of preparation has a great contribution to make to the health of everyone. Balance and harmony in diet provide a path to health that the Chinese have followed for thousands of years. Kenneth Lo, one of Britain's foremost cookery experts, presents clearly the cooking methods and principles that make Chinese food so delicious, so simple and so good for the body. And there is no better advertisement for Chinese cooking for health than Kenneth Lo himself – well into his sixties, still winning tennis championships, and still a discerning and enthusiastic diner.

£1.25

INDIAN COOKERY
by E. P. VEERASAWMY

E. P. Veerasawmy's *Indian Cookery* is already an established classic. As well as a wide range of recipes for meat and fish curries, it contains all the information you need to make Pillaus and Birianis, Kormas, Kababs, Vindaloos, Chupatties and other breads, fresh chutneys and Indian sweets. The skill and clarity with which these dishes are described gives ample evidence that Mr Veerasawmy was one of the foremost Indian chefs of the century. His book is filled with lucid tips on how the Western cook can make the most of one of India's most subtle and tasteful arts.

£1.25